BARACK HUSSEIN OBAMA:

BARACK HUSSEIN OBAMA:

OUR NEW MESSIAH ?

CHARLES H. DOERSAM, JR

TATE PUBLISHING & *Enterprises*

The New Messiah?

Published by Tate Publishing & Enterprises, LLC
127 E. Trade Center Terrace | Mustang, Oklahoma 73064 USA
1.888.361.9473 | www.tatepublishing.com

Tate Publishing is committed to excellence in the publishing industry. The company reflects the philosophy established by the founders, based on Psalm 68:11,
"The Lord gave the word and great was the company of those who published it."

Published in the United States of America

ISBN: 978-1-61739-030-2
Political Science / Political Ideologies
10.08.03

DEDICATION

To all the Chicago libs who installed him.

The arrival of liberal/Socialist/Marxist Society in the USA! Will it work here?

ACKNOWLEDGMENTS

Macht, Wiske, Kneedler, Lombard, Gaudio, Chuck, Donna, Dean, Kristen, Garvey, Lynch.

CONTENTS

AUTHOR'S NOTE

This book was written especially for the some one hundred and fifty million Americans who voted for President Obama and are now wondering if that was a really good idea after all.

It will also be eagerly sought after by the almost one hundred and fifty million Americans who did not vote for him, but who are even more concerned about the direction in which he is taking us and our children for generations to come.

And then there are the three hundred million additional, even more eager readers: the young children of all those voters.

Did I overlook interested readers in Germany, England, even France, Japan, and possibly even China?

I hope each and every one of you read it all and find it stimulating and interesting.

Isn't it great to be a participant in this, the Democratic Process, to live with freedom, in an economy that flourishes with the free enterprise system that promotes innovation and enables new enterprises to form and flourish?

Contrast this with Marxist/Socialism: that has always failed, whenever, and wherever it has been tried.

The only ones who benefit from Marxist/Socialism are the megalomaniac dictators.

And look what happened to Adolph, Benito, Joseph,

and all of the others. Mr. President, are you sure you want to walk in their Marxist/Socialist path?

Let's preserve our free enterprise system by all participating like never before in the next elections!

PREFACE

Barack Hussein Obama has won election as our president at a very young age, with no executive experience, and thirteen years as a "Community Organizer" as his major career experience.

Many Americans (including the press, both print and video) can hardly say enough great things about this new president, who has spent more of our money in his first three months than all of our previous presidents combined, in each of their full terms, summed up from the beginning of the USA.

This book examines how this happened; what is presently going on; where we are heading; and how long it will take for us to realize what is happening and set about correcting this disastrous situation.

The polls indicate that the realization is already gaining momentum.

This book is intended to accelerate that process. It seeks to make each and every reader more fully aware of what is really happening, and exactly what that means for each and everyone of us.

This guy is not really the second coming that some, especially in the press, seem to believe.

PART I:

BO's Campaign Promises *before He "Took Charge"*

Which ones can you remember?

How about these as a starter:

1. Cut taxes for 95% of all Americans making less than $250,000.00, (but that limit worked down. (Was the "bottom" $125,000.00?), so as to tax only the "rich."
2. Close GITMO
3. End the war
4. Find and "prosecute" the leader of the Taliban.
5. Talk peace with all the leaders of the nations around the world that are threatening us.
6. Bring all the troops home
7. Change, change, change

Sounds great: Peace and prosperity for all in a world where we are universally loved. Perhaps that is why he was elected.

CHAPTER ONE

THE 2008 PRESIDENTIAL ELECTION:

I Won

Your party won and my party lost. So I will hug my elephant and you can kiss your ass.

As I write this, we are less than a month into the new president and commander-in-chief installing himself in the White House, complete with mother-in-law and extended family.

But what else can you do except laugh at this whole orchestrated take over by our lib Chicago Democratic machine?

Give him a chance. Great idea, I'm in favor of that. The jury is still out, to be sure, but the counts that they are deliberating seem to be "No Brainers" (see the following chapters).

Let's take a look at the election first, to see if we can figure out why he won. But first, in keeping with the well-established democratic tradition of referring to all of their favorite presidents by their initials, such as FDR, JFK, and LBJ, tradition dictates that the new one be designated as "BO."

Since we are not allowed to mention that his middle name is Hussein, the new designator has only two characters. We must be politically correct about these matters, at all times, you know. Sooner or later, the new appellation "BO" will be universally accepted, even by the liberal press. It is obviously an appropriate designation, especially for those of us old enough to remember the life buoy first anti-body odor soap radio commercials, that had the two-note fog horn signaling: Bee Oh.

Yes, he is our new president, and the libs are saying, "Let's give him a chance." Certainly I am in favor of that, except for one little detail: it seems he wants to spend us into a permanent Socialist/liberal/Marxist society that it is going to deliberately bankrupt the economy, destroy free enterprise, and will prove to be very difficult to reverse.

I am not in favor of that. In fact, I am against it.

So let's wake up and start fighting back for a change! A real change.

Back to the subject of the election: it wasn't the "landslide" that BO would like you to think that it was. In fact, it was very close, not withstanding the reported massive efforts of the democratic machine in Chicago and ACORN to register the dead and to register the live ones at as many different polling places as they could afford, with their billion dollar plus campaign fund from, as of to date, largely undisclosed sources.

Sarah Palin was a breath of fresh air in the campaign. Did you notice that she was the only one of the four campaigners who had solid and directly applicable executive experience? McCain was second with some, but none at all in the winning democratic team of BO and Joe Biden.

As an aside: I just noticed that whenever I try to

type democratic, it somehow comes out demoncratic! (Spiritual forces playing games again?)

Did you also notice in the campaign that slogans such as: "Change change, change, we will never have change until we have change" and "Yes We Can" were repeated over and over. Isn't that exactly the same way that Adolph, Joseph, and Benito took over?

And why would you want to change an administration that created the Department of Homeland Security that has successfully protected us from any further terrorist attacks here at home, when we are at war with those very same terrorists worldwide?

And why would you want to change the very same, so vilified Bush Administration that inherited a recession, which it quickly turned into fifty-four months of economic growth and prosperity?

It was only after BO started talking about "The worst economy since the Great Depression," and, "unless we act right now...we may never be able to recover," during the last two years of the Bush presidency that the economy headed south! BO most certainly contributed heavily to that downturn, if not indeed actually precipitating it single handedly.

The scientific method says: "Postulate an outcome, and then see if you can prove it by factual observation." Let's just postulate that BO is intent on taking over the economy of the USA, or perhaps the entire world, and turning it into a liberal/Socialist/Marxist state. How would he accomplish that transition?

Look at his actions (not his words), and then you will realize how real this possibility is.

The "Economic Stimulus" Bill and the other government "assistance programs" are nothing less than the government taking over our economy permanently. That's called Marxist Socialism!

These "recovery" packages, which he has propagated with Nancy, Harry, and his other helpers, are exactly that. And as I type these words, it is about to be passed, and most likely signed into law by BO!

First step to Marxist Socialism? You bet, a very big, and very dangerous first step!

CHAPTER TWO

WHO IS THIS BO?

What are his qualifications?

During the campaign, a whole lot of questions were asked, but never asked by the press or answered by BO viz: Where was he born? Who were his parents? Is he an American citizen, born in the USA, and as such, is he eligible to be President of the United States of America?

And just what are the assigned duties of a "Community Organizer"? What did he accomplish, and how well did BO perform as one of many "Community Organizers" during his thirteen years in that role? This was his only sustained "professional" experience.

When he was apparently picked up by the Chicago democratic machine and greased into their state legislature, what was he supposed to do? And what did he actually accomplish, besides voting "present" on some 141 issues?

During his year and a third as a US Senator, when he wasn't absent and out campaigning, what did he accomplish as a senator from the great state of Illinois?

During the campaign, he repeatedly said, "I have a plan," but never divulged what that plan was. Did he really have a plan or was he just faking it? Where did he go to school? Some vague references to Harvard Law, but with distinction? What really happened there? Harvard seems mute on or almost ashamed of the subject.

How about undergraduate school? Columbia seems to be even less enthusiastic than Harvard. And who paid for this expensive education at Columbia and Harvard? And how about high school and grammar school? Any promise there?

To co-opt one of BO's favorite teleprompter reading expressions: "Bottom line," it seems that this guy doesn't have a clue about what to do in his newly acquired position of president of the USA.

I forgot about illegal drugs. Was he a "free enterprise" pusher or just a user, as he describes?

He seems totally unaware of what the Constitution says about the duties and the powers of the president and the limitations on those powers. But he, in his own mind, will be "the boss" and fix everything, single-handedly. He is the *boss*, no two ways about it. In fact, it seems that he thinks he already has the dictatorial powers that he seeks and apparently expected to come with the new job.

He is in for a whole lot of surprises.

Humble he is not. He proclaims, "It is I who will make all of the decisions." He is a very dangerous, completely deceptive man who has fooled a whole lot of hardworking Americans. He is intent on stripping them of their life savings, so that he, BO, can be the *boss* in perpetuity.

When FDR was pressing for an amendment to our constitution, permitting him to run for a *third* term, and we were voting on whether or not to accept that as a modification to our constitution, emotions on the subject were running high. It was then that my classmate, Johnnie Pollak, came to school one day with a huge button, proclaiming: "No *Fourth* Term!"

Funny? Yes, but this BO is further to the left than all the other libs in the Congress and in the Democratic Party, in the history of our great United States of America.

With a reported fifteen billion to ACORN, and more to his other handlers, it is quite possible that when he creates enough dependent, loving, Socialists/Marxists, that he will be able to pass just such an amendment...enabling him, the "Messiah," to stay in power forever!

That's fifteen billion dollars with a "B." Do you have any idea how much that is? If you counted full-time as fast as you can, from birth to death, your entire life, you might reach twenty million. Each of those fifteen billion, destined for ACORN, is a thousand million!

BO, like all politicians, does not forget his friends. But here comes dear old BO, and one of his very first moves is to grab fifteen billion for his buddies at ACORN.

There is still an awful lot that we don't know about our new president. But what we do know is indeed frightening.

Why do you suppose that the liberal biased "news" media fails to explore and or expand on these questions? That is supposed to be their job. Why aren't they doing it?

Just maybe the schools that they went to also indoctrinated them on the "virtues" of Marxist/Socialist/liberal politics. And perhaps they actually believe that capitalism, big business, Halliburton, Bush, Cheney, are all evil. After all, they repeat it over and over and over, ad nauseum. (Perhaps that is why the liberal press, print, and video are going out of business? Downsizing: First step. To oblivion? Seems very likely.)

And thank God for *Fox News* and all of the talk radio shows that have honest up-to-the-minute real news of what is actually happening, not just what the lib censors want to filter and release, in the same way that propaganda was generated by Joe, Adolph, Benito, and all of the other failed dictators.

But the liberal press never tells us *why* the capital-driven free enterprise system championed by Bush and Cheney is bad. The very same free enterprise capital system that has made this the greatest country in the world. They just keep repeating that it is "evil," in their "news," over and over again. Sort of like BO's, "Change, Change, Change! We will never have change until we have change!"

And yet there were people who perhaps thought that that was a good idea. They voted for him. I wonder if they still feel that way now, after they have had their first glimpse of what that "Pig in the Poke," that they bought (without knowing what it really was) really looks like.

It will be fun to see what happens in the next elections. Don't forget to be there early and often if you are in support of free enterprise.

PART II:

BO's Actions Critiqued After He "Took Charge"

It is still early, to be sure. We are still in those magical first hundred days, but there is a clear pattern emerging. Let's have a look at it:

1. BO is still promising to cut those taxes for 95% of the taxpayers. *Dream on. I can assure you that will never happen. Taxes are going up. Way up. Yours and all the rest of us, rich and poor alike; and that includes everyone in the "middle" as well. Yes, up, way up for years to come. For one and all!*
2. He signed an Executive Order on day one, just as he promised, to close GITMO in a year at the latest. *Oops! And now he belatedly discovers that some, if not all, of those prisoners' countries of origin* do not *want those guys back. Big surprise? Some clever entrepreneurs in Great Brittan, and even in Germany, are saying perhaps that they could take care of a few of them for a substantial price (of course). In the meantime, the finest prison in the world, established by our navy, is scheduled to be shut down in a year. I say keep it open. We may need it for future terrorists from right here at home.*
3. End the war. "Whoops," it will take a little longer, and by the way, we need more troops in Afghanistan! *He seems to be encountering problems in keeping that "promise" too. And on the subject of war, our potential attackers from all over the world are reacting to BO's weakness on military intentions by rattling their collective sabers louder than ever before. Is "peace" at any cost working as well as BO expected?*

4. Find Bin Laden. Still looking; but be assured that when we do, we will "prosecute him." *Be sure that the arresting officer reads him his rights before you take him away! Don't you just love these libs? How about just shooting the bastard? Or in feel-good lib speak: How about dispatching him instead, to meet those twenty-seven virgins, (now mushroomed to seventy-two, like all good lib promises)?*
5. Talk peace with all the bad guys all around the world. He is well on his way on his rounds of apologizing for the "evil" USA all over the place. *How well is that working out?*
6. Bring all the troops home. Whoops, that will take a little while, and by the way we need more in Afghanistan, so I am sending more there right away. But I am drastically cutting the defense budget, starting with F-22 production. *This prompts the question: Does he have a clue about what our Armed Forces do? Perhaps a little tour of duty, following basic training, or better yet, boot camp, might be helpful?*
7. Stop the war. See above! *And with threats mushrooming all around the world. When weakness is evident, it encourages attack. And this guy is advertising his weakness. For one: he has proclaimed that he wants to reduce the nuclear arsenal, with the ultimate objective of eliminating all nuclear capability around the world. How is that for "blood" in the water? Watch out: here come the sharks!*

8. Change, change, change. This is in full swing. *But is it the change that you really expected?*

The chapters that follow take a closer look at what is happening as a result of BO moving in to our White House. He seems to think that we work for him, and therefore he can dictate our every move. I have news for him. It's the other way around. He is supposed to work for us.

As you read on, ask yourself: Is this the change I really want? Do I really want to just sit back and be totally stripped of all initiative? Do I really want Big Brother deciding how much I can earn, and how much I can keep? And all those other controls on our day-to-day lives that even tell us how much water we can use to flush our toilets?

CHAPTER THREE

THE ECONOMIC DOWNTURN

"The worst since the Great Depression?"

In lib speak, he will blame Bush and say: "I inherited it." Maybe so, but he certainly contributed heavily to its growth during his two-year campaign. And his early actions seem to be deliberately directed toward intentionally further exacerbating a self-contrived downward plunge.

Yes, the economy is down. What do you expect after a two-year BO campaign in which he constantly drummed away at "The worst economy since the Great Depression," and, "An economic crisis that we may never be able to recover from."

Remember, libs agree with what they have been told by other libs, especially when the other lib is BO, their new "Messiah." Yes, in lib speak he will blame Bush and say, "I inherited that."

Maybe so, but he certainly contributed heavily to its growth during the campaign. And his early actions seem to be deliberately directed toward further exacerbating it.

Remember FDR's famous quote: "We have nothing to fear but fear itself"? It seems the libs may have as their primary objective purposively ditching the economy to create a crisis, so that they can install more and more of their onerous regulations, raise taxes, and spend, spend, spend!

I forgot to add so that they can grab power and retain, "Dictatorial control…forever!" Isn't that the same way that Adolf, Benito, Joseph, and all of those guys in other dictatorships and Marxist/Socialist countries "solved" the problem? How well did that work out?

The government cannot spend us out of an economic downturn. It does not help. It makes matters worse. Much worse. It seems liberals just want to "feel" good about what they are doing. It doesn't really matter what the end result is, as long as they are doing "something" about it!

See the next chapters!

CHAPTER FOUR

THE ECONOMIC "STIMULUS"

BO's Marxists/Socialist "Solution"

Do you know what a "googolplex" is? It is the creation of a mathematician to illustrate the enormity of the concept of "infinity." He defined it as ten to the tenth power, to the tenth power, to the tenth power, on and on, forever!

Perhaps BO thinks that the US Treasury is equipped with a googolplex, an endless supply of dollars.

This is appropriate, because our newly installed figure head of the apparently Marxist/Socialist "Democratic" Party, BO, seems to think that you can spend your way out of a recession.

Herbert Hoover conceived that idea. It got us further into trouble. FDR perpetuated that idea, and that is why for seven years or more the economic downturn was perpetuated.

It does not work. It makes things worse. Much worse!

BO seems to be confused between creating "jobs," and creating "work." There is a difference. A very big difference. The government can create all manner of "work" to fix infrastructure. But when it's fixed, that's the end of it.

Free enterprise creates jobs to grow and prosper, and those jobs are permanent, for as long as the free enterprise flourishes and is not stifled to death by more and more stupid and onerous, inhibiting government regulation.

See the difference?

All we need are tax cuts, across the board. That approach has never failed, and when Ronald Regan implemented it we had the longest period of sustained economic prosperity in our history.

The other thing we can do is reduce the federal and state payrolls. Those guys never yet have produced a single dollar of gross domestic product. They are a drain on our very existence. Cut them to the bone and pass the savings to the military to let the world know that we mean business!

During the campaign, BO said that he was going to "Go through the entire budget, line by line, and eliminate all the waste." Sounded great, even without the line item veto, which would allow him to carry out that (fake) promise. But what happened when he won?

He evidently delegated the preparation of the entire "plan" to Nancy Pelosi and Harry Reid, apparently with the executive order: "Make it at least a trillion and a half! And be sure to include ACORN!"

What came out is a plethora of pet projects, some fifteen hundred pages long, that contains more waste and "pork" than anything, except perhaps fifteen billion for ACORN. There are over four thousand wasteful "pork" projects in that bill, and I will bet that BO hasn't even read it, despite his pledge to "eliminate all waste."

And BO is right there, as if he were still on the campaign trail, proclaiming: "We must pass this right now. If we wait, it may be too late, and we may never recover."

How stupid does he think that we are? (Perhaps we are. We elected him.)

BO lies. Freedom dies!

"No pork?" It is almost all pork!

"We must pass this right now; to stimulate the economy!"

He breaks his word: "You will have a minimum of forty-eight hours to read and understand what is in it." (All fifteen hundred pages…) And instead of the promised forty-eight hours, they rammed it through in the dead of the night of that very same day!

I can guarantee you that not a single one of those congressmen, in the House or in the Senate, had the time or the ability to read and understand that bill before Nancy and Harry jammed it through the Congress and "passed" it, before any of the members of Congress realized what they were doing to our future. None of them, obviously, had any idea about what was in it and what they had done.

For that matter neither did Harry Reid, Nancy Pelosi, BO, or anyone of the long list of pork generators understand the entire package and its significance to our future. Is that the sort of completely irresponsible government you expected when you voted for BO? I certainly hope not. But that's what we now have.

Remember to choose wisely in 2010. It will be here before you know it.

What else can be done about it? They should all be impeached and jailed for high treason. If they had had time to read it and understand it, I seriously doubt if even the far left libs would have voted for it.

Despite BO's repeated proclamations that "there is no pork in this bill," there are about *four thousand different pork projects*. He lies. The spending is slow to start, in spite of the big rush to pass it. The spending peaks in 2010, which just happens to be the next Congressional election year.

Coincidence? Or intentional?

Time for a change?

A real change this time?

You bet.

Don't forget to vote in 2010 and 2012 too.

CHAPTER FIVE

CONTROL DETROIT?

Regulate, Manage, Dictate, and Destroy!

Detroit is experiencing financial difficulties. Let's consider why this may be. Their labor problem was created not by management but by the unions who demanded so much more than the companies could afford that the companies are being strangled by the union-generated extra costs.

And just how did the unions develop this all-powerful position?

You guessed it if you asked: Could it be by government regulations that the unions promoted by generous monetary "campaign" contributions to those in the government who then make those onerous regulations?

The foreign car makers have avoided this. They are very competitive as a result.

BO needs to remove those union-inspired laws and regulations and watch Detroit swiftly recover.

Oh, did I forget an even more urgent action for BO? Get rid of the other performance regulations so that the automobile manufactures are free to conceive and market the automobiles that their buyers need and want. And while you are at it, BO, get rid of the onerous government regulations and mandates on education. As a "bonus," education will recover, too!

Detroit has a problem with their product as well. There are a whole lot of requirements that have been mandated by these government regulations. They must meet all of them. Some of those requirements directly conflict with each other. The list is long and onerous, but let me give you a sample.

One requirement is that the fuel economy, in miles per gallon, must meet ever increasing "mandates"! Another requirement is that the product has to comply with ever more demanding "safety standards." Both of these regulations make libs "feel" like such really good people who truly "care."

Now fuel economy is achieved by reducing the weight of the vehicle, and safety is achieved by increasing the weight of the vehicle!

Let's take a look at another example: in the name of "saving the planet," from (the non-existent), "man-made global warming," the permitted emission of those evil "greenhouse" gasses has been progressively reduced. This has resulted in the addition of catalytic converters to the exhaust system, thereby increasing cost by close to a thousand dollars with little or no effect on the environment.

In order to skirt the fuel economy regulations and satisfy the safety regulations, while complying with the emission regulations, and a whole host of other regulations, that we don't even want to know about: the auto manufacturers were very creative indeed. They noticed that "trucks" were not subject to those onerous fuel economy regulations. So they simply put a few seats in a box "truck" body, on a light truck chassis, and *presto!* No more fuel economy standards.

The problem of selling a "truck" to a customer seeking an "automobile" was "solved" by an equally creative marketing move. They simply renamed it a "Sports Utility Vehicle," or "SUV." Sounds great. You have to run out and buy one of those!

This is a typical liberal way of disguising what they are really up to. Names such as "stimulus" for government engaging in grabbing control is yet another example. Yes, the "news" used to report "An SUV rolled over…" But no more. "Political correctness" got that squared away. Now it's a "vehicle" rolled over.

Have you noticed?

It is yet another example of how this socialist inspired "political correctness" has intruded into, and permeated, our society. They want to tell us what we can do and what we cannot do or say at every turn in our lives.

Is indoctrinating us to accept "political correctness" just the first step (in that "plan," that BO keeps telling us that he has) to make us all follow along in lockstep, and accept the complete installation of the Marxist/ Socialism, that BO is quite obviously so intent on instigating.

I don't know about you, but I am sick of it.

I have had it.

(And that is why I am typing away on this book.)

Do you really want that? Is that what you thought you were getting when you voted for good old BO?

Wake up and take some initiative! Do something on your own for a change, a real change!

Back to those SUV trucks.

Those things really do roll over easily. What do you expect with so much sticking up so high?

That was learned way back in 1936, when cars started to be built closer to the ground, so that they would have a lower center of gravity and resist roll over.

So they now advertise, for an extra charge (of course), that your SUV can be equipped with "anti-roll" equipment! How well do you suppose that "works?" How do they lower the center of gravity? More weight downstairs? Or do they simply adjust the suspension to limit roll and give the driver the illusion of safety by reducing the feeling of imminent roll over, so that the driver doesn't realize it in time to take appropriate corrective action?

Is it possible that the "anti-roll" feature (that you pay extra for) actually increases the likelihood that you will experience a sudden and unexpected roll over?

But libs don't care if it really works or does not work. They just want to "feel" that they cared enough to do "something" about it.

That is a brief discussion of how the onerous governmental regulations created the mess in Detroit. Powerful unions with a stranglehold on struggling "free" enterprises.

Forced to produce a product that satisfies government specifications (but not their customers), and so rigorously controlled that they can no longer effectively compete with foreign car manufacturers who are free from the union burdens and only have to carry some of the regulatory burdens.

And what does BO do about it? He, "The Boss," summons them all to him, to beg for "aid," from him in front of his faithful congressional helpers. Then he fires the CEO of GM, puts Chrysler into a mock government take over called "bankruptcy," and on and on!

How do you suppose that faithful Ford Motors, managed to quietly proceed while avoiding all this mess?

(Or did they?)

No question about it, BO is the "Boss." He will fix everything, all by himself (and end up with his Socialist/Marxists government owning it all.)

What does our Constitution say about all of those precipitous presidential actions? Are they impeachable offenses? What other recourse do we have? Better keep GITMO open, just in case we may need it.

And by the way, he has already passed a law that retroactively effectively nullifies bonuses in the financial industries that traditionally use them to stimulate initiative and reward productivity.

Back to Detroit. What he has already enacted is far from helpful. It is downright destructive. Could it be that he is intentionally destroying our major industries, one by one? Is that what you guys in Detroit expected when you voted for this new Messiah?

And all you other libs not from Detroit, look out; you may be next on this massive Marxist/Socialist power grab.

CHAPTER SIX

BO'S APPROACH TO ENERGY

The fuel that Energizes our Economy!

Yes, it is the driving force that energizes our economy. But dear old BO has not yet realized this.

In the following chapters, we will address various aspects of the energy problem, with a view toward educating BO on what needs to be done and why his vaguely described proclamations are flawed, speaking politely, and how, in fact, they will destroy our nation when and if he is successful in implementing them, speaking more directly.

It's becoming more and more apparent that BO doesn't have a clue about what to do in his new position as president of the United States of America. With respect to energy, this is particularly true.

BO is pushing for the "long range solutions" for our energy needs. Energy derived from wind, solar, geothermal, electric car, and "battery."

In fact, during the campaign both of the presidential candidates advocated that approach.

The difference is that BO seems to think that he, the boss, can order it, and it will magically, instantly happen!

It doesn't work that way, Mr. President!

There are fundamental laws of physics and engineering that limit what even you cannot overrule.

Even with a realistic goal, it takes a lot of hard Research and Development work. That R and D work takes time, and costs a whole lot of money.

Time we do not have. Lots of money is something that BO likes. It apparently gives him a feeling of power, as he happily spends our money.

To think that this R and D can be quickly accomplished simply because he, BO, mandates it, clearly demonstrates a complete lack of understanding of basic physics and engineering.

That "green" energy that you are promoting, even if you throw gazillions of dollars at it in wasted R and D efforts, is a long way off, ten to twenty years at least.

Energy is needed now, to power our economy, not maybe "green" energy in ten to twenty years!

And when, if ever, BO's green energy emerges, guess what? When (and if) it ever arrives it will be a long way from being economically viable. The only way that successful R and D generates an economically viable new product is when free enterprise is unshackled from onerous government regulations. Period.

The "government" doesn't do well in this sort of R and D effort. In fact, they have a miserable track record. Let me give you a specific example: solar energy.

Perhaps it was forty or more years ago that the Department of Energy, "DOE," tried to promote solar energy by means of a massively funded "stimulus" package. It was a dismal failure (just like all government sponsored stimulus packages, past, present, and future). It simply does not work.

Here's what happened to the DOE solar effort. The approach was to give every homeowner a payment of some four hundred dollars when they purchased an "approved" solar collector and installed it on their property. And what was required to manufacture an "approved" solar collector? You guessed it: It had to comply with DOE specifications. Get the idea? Control, control, control!

Well, one of the DOE specs. required that the solar collector be "efficient." Sounds reasonable, right? Except for one little detail, they also very specifically "defined efficiency," as heat in BTU-generated per *square foot of sunlight.*

In order to meet this specification, all of the newly created suppliers produced products that were way too expensive, for the heat collection capacity that they provided. They were *not economically* "efficient," and they were therefore not economically viable. There was no market for the product. It was not economically viable. It was DOA.

Sunlight is plentiful. There is no need to "conserve" it.

If you define "efficiency" as BTU produced *per dollar cost*, instead of per square foot of sunlight, you easily come up with an economically viable commercial product.

Private, unsubsidized, free enterprise came up with just such an alternate, and that was much more effective. It was a black rubber bladder, with passageways for circulating water, and you simply laid it on your roof, where it was exposed to sunlight.

It cost about one-tenth of the cost of the "approved" models.

A number of very creative builders have gone even further. They simply put a coil of flexible black plastic pipe in the sun. Works well too. It costs even less.

Free enterprise at work. Get the idea? Economic viability drives the success of any new product. Without it, it dies, just as Marxist/Socialism has failed everywhere it has been forced on people.

Only a legitimate identified market need will inspire the creation of successful new and innovative, economically viable, products to satisfy that need. Free enterprise creates new products that are enthusiastically purchased and enjoyed by everyone (who needs them, and can afford them.) That is how capitalism works! And that is why it is so successful!

Compare that record with the Marxist/Socialism, that BO is perpetrating.

It's called "free enterprise." It works. With no "assistance" from the government. It works. It works well.

Presently, the DOE and other government agencies are heavily supporting solid state methods for generating electricity directly from sunlight.

Yes, they are screwing up yet another time.

These are very interesting. We have a "solar" powered "garden light" that has solid state solar collectors, and multiple solid state light-emitting diode lamp elements. It glows ever so elegantly during evenings, after bright sunshine days have charged its little battery.

Great? Pretty, but you could not see to read even a label with it. Its cost, even at the "low, low bargain close-out prices," was about a factor of a hundred from being financially viable as a practical source of illumination on a commercial scale.

Some of "big business" has already installed massive solid-state solar arrays of these things on the roofs of their New York City skyscrapers, at obviously very high capital cost.

The "benefits" derived there from are primarily a reinforcement of their "green" PR image, to show that "We Care."

Incidentally, the maintenance cost to keep these things working is substantial. It includes removing the dirt, crud, and bird droppings left behind by the pigeons, and the smoke from the fossil-fuel-burning heating systems in their own building and in their neighbors' buildings.

The power output that these massive solar arrays produce is more than from our garden light, but it is still only way less than one percent of their building's power requirement.

Sure you want to go there, BO? Get yourself a scientific advisor who knows what he is doing. Trust him, before you go off once again, half cocked, and make ever more foolish declarations.

CHAPTER SEVEN

BATTERIES

The Dumbest Idea of All!

The dumbest idea of all as a *source* for renewable energy is the "Battery" championed by both Obama and his opponent during his campaign. They both suggested that a "Battery" is actually a source of energy.

A battery that can be recharged is a storage device for electrical energy, not a source. Whatever you put in,you get out, almost. Not all of it comes back. Some is lost.

Disposable "dry cells" that are not storage batteries do produce electricity by interaction between the chemicals that they contain. They quit when all the chemicals have interacted and are depleted. That is most certainly not a potential source for viable commercial energy.

The "hybrid" automobile is an interesting concept. As originally proposed, it was configured with a battery capacity intended only to store power, generated as the vehicle went down hills. During that time, instead of dissipating power as heat, in the required braking, a power generator would absorb the power and slow the vehicle instead of dissipating that power as waste heat in the brakes.

Similarly, when going up steep hills, the power

stored in the battery (from going down hill braking) would be available to assist the engine in maintaining speed, going up hill.

In this way, a smaller, more efficient engine would always be operating within its most efficient speed range. In addition, the power that is normally dissipated as heat in the brakes is captured for future use, thereby increasing fuel economy!

To accomplish these objectives, the design of the original "Marco Polo" hybrid automobile was conceived in the early 1950s. The Marco Polo included other innovative concepts, including all-wheel drive, computer-controlled pulsed rotary drive actuators on each of its wheels, a directional control that was digital, and it used a joystick instead of a steering wheel for directional control by individual wheel incremental control actuation instead of pivoting the wheels by turning a steering wheel.

Acceleration and speed were also controlled with the same joystick. Speed and turning rates were automatically regulated (restricted by the computer) to *prevent* roll over.

The net result was a car designed for lower cost of acquisition and operation, improved mileage per gallon, and greater safety, which could be manufactured easily, efficiently, economically, sold at a very attractive low price, and yield substantial profit to its manufacturer.

Unfortunately, this concept vehicle was never launched because its inventor was (at that time) unfamiliar with capital sources and how to get the necessary capital investment needed to launch a company.

But the concept is still valid, still there, and still as

economically viable as ever. And the original inventor is still here and ready to go. (Me!)

The "hybrids" we see in today's market have attempted to do a few of the same things. The problem is that they are using a larger battery, a more expensive battery, which adds weight and initial cost as well as an extremely high replacement cost when it craps out.

That is not what the public market wants.

The "hybrids" on the market today also lack the other features that make Marco Polo a manufacturer's dream to produce. Features necessary to make it an economically viable product (In addition their poor performance). The Marco Polo design, by contrast, can be readily scaled to high-performance sport car agility, or conservative family economy car, using the same design and major components.

In short, the "hybrid" automobiles presently available are not what the public desperately needs.

With Detroit hard at work with any sort of dumb luck the Marco Polo will re-emerge in due course, sooner or later triumphantly! And the inventor is still available to assist!

Free enterprise works. Socialism does not. It never will, no matter how hard BO tries to force it on us so that he and he alone can be "The Boss" forever!

CHAPTER EIGHT

NUCLEAR FISSION

BO Needs to Learn More About this Too!

This is our presently available best source for clean, efficient, inexpensive energy. Nuclear fission is here and now. It is economically viable, in fact, very profitable, and it is safe.

Ask the Germans, the French, the other countries in Europe, and Scandinavia, China, Japan, and Russia, who all have nuclear power plants, as does the US Navy.

But alas, BO doesn't, as yet, understand this. Perhaps his new scientific advisor can explain this to him, too, so that the ban on constructing new nuclear power plants in the USA will be lifted.

Let me give it a try.

The word "nuclear" to a lib seems to be the same as "Nuclear Bomb." There is a difference. To make a nuclear bomb, you simply, very rapidly jam sufficient nuclear material together to form a "critical mass" that goes boom. That "nuclear material" is highly enriched material, enriched for the express purpose of making it go boom with as much blast as possible.

A nuclear power plant is totally different. It seeks to heat water to the boiling point and create steam. The steam is then used to turn steam turbines, which turn alternators that generate electrical power safely and efficiently.

Let's take a closer look. The nuclear material that is used to heat the water is not the same "enriched" fuel that is used to go boom. The heat that it can produce is controlled, so as to be extracted only as needed.

The key word here is "controlled."

The Russians had a gigantic nuclear "Oops," at Chernobyl. It was because they had a totally different "solution" to the controlled release of the heat, which obviously did not work. It got too hot. So hot that it melted its enclosure: a "meltdown."

That failed control method is no longer used in any of the many nuclear power plants, that are operating so successfully, safely, and economically all around the world.

Let's repeat (for BO, and for all of his lib boosters). A nuclear reaction in a power plant is not the same as a nuclear reaction in a nuclear detonation.

The reaction in the power plant is a carefully controlled extraction of heat to boil water and make steam. The needed heat is very carefully extracted from radioactive material. That heat is utilized to turn alternators in the same way that heat from burning fossil fuels is used for the same purpose.

The second fear that some people have is the Russian Chernobyl incident. What they don't understand is that the Russian design of that plant was quite different. It failed. It got too hot. Radioactive material escaped.

With the designs now operating in Russia, throughout the world in the ships and boats at sea this cannot happen. It is difficult to convince a lib of anything.

They have a tendency to absolutely accept only whatever they have been told (from another lib).

This is a preview, BO, of what your new Scientific Advisor will provide for you. Let's build nuclear power plants.

You can be a real hero. Solve the problem. Don't just talk about how great it is going to be.

CHAPTER NINE

NUCLEAR FUSION

The Real Deal, but a Ways Off!

Nuclear fusion, as a source of virtually unlimited clean energy, is truly the real deal when and if it can ever be achieved. It is the same nuclear reaction that powers our sun and all of the other "suns" in our universe.

Nuclear fusion, in theory, says that if you jam two hydrogen atoms together in a controlled manner they will both disappear and yield the inherent energy in their mass. The energy produced will be very substantial indeed.

In the immortal equation of Albert Einstein, "E" the amount of energy released, is equal to the mass "M" of the two hydrogen atoms, times the speed of light "C" raised to the second power E= M x C^2.

Even though the mass of the two hydrogen atoms is miniscule, that last term is pretty large, and when you square it, it is truly an enormous number.

For well over thirty years, work on this source of energy has been progressing at the Princeton University's "Plasma Physics Laboratory," as well as several government DOE controlled laboratories. Progress is steady and encouraging.

More recently, the French embarked on a huge similar plasma project, also designed to achieve controlled, sustained production of energy by means of nuclear fusion. It is progressing well, too.

Even more recently, the Lawrence Livermore Laboratory in California has announced progress on smaller, more carefully controlled approaches that appear to be on the verge of a major breakthrough. They utilize photons from a very powerful system of *lasers* to initiate and sustain controlled nuclear fusion.

There is an interesting statistic on nuclear fusion, which says: "A bottle of hydrogen gas will satisfy all of the power needs of New York City for over a hundred years." And it is safe, clean, economically viable energy!

BO should have one of his handlers load that one in one of his many teleprompters. A word to BO: act on it, and act wisely, after you are thoroughly informed.

CHAPTER TEN

OIL AND NATURAL GAS

It's Here Now; Burns Clean, Too!

There is another source of energy that is also here now. It's called "oil." We have an abundant supply, and we need to use it while we are building new nuclear powered power plants.

Natural gas comes from the same drilling prospect holes. Sometimes it is all gas, sometimes it comes with oil, and sometimes it is only oil. But natural gas and oil are both very rich sources of energy that need to be utilized, just as our other sources of energy need to be utilized.

When you believe in God, you understand that God put them here to be utilized.

Energy is the driving engine of our economy. Why do you suppose the libs want to impede its discovery and utilization? Their "Stop Global Warming," and "Save the Planet" bumper sticker arguments have already been proven to be totally false and self-contrived to enable them to grab more and more control.

In order to use oil and natural gas we need to find it. To find it, we need to lift the onerous restrictions on drilling on and offshore.

Why should we sit idly by and do no drilling while China is drilling off our shore on behalf of Castro-land? Extracting oil and/or gas from a single ocean platform, with a series of radial drill holes, is effective, efficient, safe, and non-polluting.

What reason could possibly be given to justify restricting the USA from finding and using this valuable natural resource, the natural resource that powers our economy?

The alternative is not attractive, but our lib friends have not as yet figured that out. Come to think about that, they do not ever figure things out. They believe only what they have been told by other libs.

Have you ever visited an oil refinery? It is a very exciting experience. Especially when you are in high school! See my book on the Lincoln School (plug!). Our lib friends do not permit the construction of new oil refineries either. We need them, too. New ones are more efficient and they make more money. More money for "Big Oil" results in more exploration, more jobs, more oil, less dependence on those guys in the Middle East, lower prices at the pump, and greater military security for the USA and its allies.

Wake up time, BO.

Did I forget to mention that it also drives the economy for the benefit of all Americans?

Lift those onerous restrictions and let us rev up our economy.

That would be real change. You would be a real hero with such an awakening. Not just a make-believe want-to-be hero because "you care." Or was that Bill who cared? BO is the man of action. Problem seems to be he acts on impulse, impulse apparently instilled by education in a liberal Marxist/Socialist educational environment, and with twenty years in a church very angry against all white "oppression."

These inner feelings that he is holding back sometimes leak out implicitly, as clearly demonstrated in his press conference attacking the white officer of the Cambridge Police force for arresting the black professor, who was causing a bit of a problem!

And all he has to do is say, "I made a mistake," and apologize.

To date he hasn't. Libs always want to seem to be right. Is there a documented incidence of any lib ever apologizing for any action?

Just think, BO, you could lead the way if you apologized to that white police officer in Bean town!

CHAPTER ELEVEN

COAL

It's Here Now, and Burns Clean Too!

There is another fuel that is also readily available, and in plentiful supply. It is called "coal," and its use is also strangled by onerous governmental regulations.

Sure enough, in the past, coal was sometimes burned less efficiently, and it did produce smoke. Now the power companies that burn coal do not want to waste any of their fuel either. After all, they paid for it; they want it to burn; not allow it to go up the chimney as unburned fuel, otherwise known as "smoke." Real, honest, black "smoke."

In the case of coal, just as with oil, when it burns completely it produces water vapor that emerges from the smoke stacks as billowy white clouds of what liberals identify (incorrectly) as "smoke." This is *not* the aforementioned black smoke. This is *not* a pollutant. It is the water vapor that is one of the natural products of *complete* combustion. The very same water that we humans need to drink in order to exist on this planet.

But try to tell that one to a lib! They frequently print pictures of massive, billowing clouds of steam, condensed water vapor, a natural product of complete combustion, and mistakenly label it as an evil pollutant!

Libs believe this. Remember, they believe everything that they are told. They are always politically correct and, oh, such good people. (In their minds only!)

While we are on the subject of water and water vapor, some of those same non-informed libs think that water is a non-renewable resource. They actually worry that some day it will be "all used up." And some day we will not have any left. Like food.

Some of those libs are actually sterilizing themselves ostensibly to "Save the Planet from over population." (Or is it really just to avoid the work and cost of raising a family? They do tend to shun any and all hard work.)

And on and on it goes. Is it impossible for them to figure things out on their own? Seems that way. We can only hope, and pray, even harder for them!

Back to coal. The power companies pay for it. They don't want to burn it inefficiently. They have an economic motivation, a strong, *competitive* motivation to produce power as inexpensively and efficiently as possible.

They use all manner of high technology means to accomplish this. And those means are impressive indeed. They work.

All manner of fossil fuels can be, and are being, burned with no pollution.

Gone are the soft-coal-burning days of the steam-driven locomotives that polluted.

It is interesting to note that when they were pulling a heavy load from standstill to start, or up a hill, that sure enough they put out black smoke that polluted.

But in power plants, the load is not intermittent. It is selectively and carefully controlled. The result is clean, efficient, effective, complete burn.

The high-tech means that enable clean, complete

burn includes fancy furnaces, high pressure boilers, all manner of auxiliary scrubbers, heat recyclers, and computer controls. All to get every last BTU (unit of heat) from each pound of coal, drop of fuel, or cubic foot of gas.

The motivation to burn clean is a financial one. Not a government-mandated restriction that rejects fossil fuels totally in favor of "green" sources or onerous regulations that need to be circumvented. Financial motivation is a real motivator. Every bit of unburned fuel is dollars going up the stack.

They don't need any governmental agency to impose restrictions on what they are doing. They can figure it out all by themselves.

That's why you will not find many good engineers who are libs.

Our coal supply is abundant, one of the largest in the world.

The technology is presently available to utilize coal efficiently without polluting the atmosphere (or any other part of the environment), and it is economically viable. *Now.*

Coal comes in three forms: Hard, soft, and shale.

Among its virtues, it can be converted into gas for more convenient storage, and later burning. In that conversion process, gas is produced along with some other very interesting and vital byproducts. In these processes, coal is also converted into pure carbon "coke." The "conversion" process also yields many other useful byproducts, which have a variety of other useful applications, including the remaining coke for burning to produce heat, just like coal.

Ask the residents of the coal-producing states, and

they will tell you about the onerous regulations that prevent the utilization of this plentiful natural resource, which is so vital to our industrial health and growth and the individual future of each and every one of us.

Then, Mr. President, sign one of your executive orders to lift those restrictions. That will do more for your poll numbers than "It's the worst economy since the Great Depression!"

Do something really useful: Remove the restrictions that prevent the use of coal, and oil, and nuclear. And then you will be a genuine hero, not just a good-looking guy.

CHAPTER TWELVE

WIND *A LA* DOE

Don't Blow It Yet Again, DOE!

Wind is also one of BO's favorite teleprompter talking points, and its true there is a lot of wind, which can, in fact, be used to contribute to the electric grid in an economically viable manner.

The problem is that when the government gets into anything, they tend to screw it up royally. Wind is no exception. Why? Here are a few of the main reasons:

1. Two-hundred-foot-high towers, equipped with three-blade aircraft-type propellers
2. Driving alternators at carefully regulated speed in order to
3. "Synchronize" to the sixty cycle grid.
4. For a cost of two million dollars per windmill!

All of that was apparently conceived and implemented by the same "scientific mentality" that "created" the "efficiency" standards for those previously described DOE solar collectors.

In short, it is not economically "efficient," and therefore not economically viable.

Yes, it most likely is "efficient," in the use of the wind, by letting most of it pass through undisturbed, but there is plenty of wind. The goal is to extract power from the wind in an economically viable manner, and these "wind farms" are most certainly not even intended to do that.

In addition to:

1. Costing a fortune, which may never be recovered from the power they produce before they die, they
2. Screw up radio transmission
3. Kill birds (and bats)
4. Make an unpleasant noise for miles around.
5. They are unsightly. Sufficiently unsightly so that even the late, "Great Senator" Kennedy, from the Great State of Massachusetts, said, "Not in my backyard, not in my view." And
6. If the grid goes down during a high-speed wind, the two million dollar windmill is in serious jeopardy of self-destruction from over speeding. Oops!

Now this entire contraption, created with your funds, by your government, is very much like the previously described abortive attempt of DOE to spur the growth and utilization of solar collectors. The result is the same. Failure economically.

Apparently BO and his team do not realize or understand how a free enterprise, capital- driven society grows and prospers.

(Just perhaps he is not in favor of growth and prosperity. Perhaps he has been so indoctrinated in radical Socialist/Marxists doctrine and is sufficiently deluded with his own grandeur, that he really believes that he, and he alone, can fix everything.)

Communism has never worked. Do you really want it installed here by BO?

"Yes, but he is so handsome. That's why I voted for him!" Is what I hear from my lib acquaintances.

No amount of government control ever produced a single dollar of gross national product.

"Profit" is a word unknown to the government, except, of course, as a target for additional taxation.

BO needs to find yet another advisor, a financial advisor who understands capitalism, and listen to him to see if he can learn and understand why capitalism is the foundation on which our great nation was founded and has thrived over these hundreds of years. We do not want to follow BO's path to government ownership and Marxist/Socialist control, with this totally clueless guy acting as our new and self-appointed dictator.

He needs to learn about free enterprise instead of just reading the Marxist material prepared by others and implanted on one or more of his multiple teleprompters.

If we thought Marxism worked, and if we wanted it, we, each and everyone of us, would have long ago moved to Cuba or elsewhere where it has been tried and failed dismally.

We don't.

It's time to stop its spread in the good old USA. Call your senators and your representatives in Congress and explain this to each and every one of them. That is how our country is supposed to work. Call, call, call! Write, write, write!

And share this book with your friends (and the libs).

CHAPTER THIRTEEN

WIND, SANS DOE

Let Innovation Freely Rein!

What is an economically viable solution to utilizing the wind for power?

Let's start with a small design, which can be attached to the roof of every homeowner who decides to buy one or more.

With an initial cost of under a thousand dollars, the device will pay for itself in two to three years (or less), depending on how much wind is at each location.

Private enterprise presently has a detailed design for just such a device. (Contact me if you want to learn more.) It works, and works well! It yields a thirty to fifty percent return on investment. Free enterprise at work!

With that kind of return, every house in the land will have one or more spinning away and driving their electric meters backward. With that return on investment, just throw it away two or three years after it arrives, when and if it ever needs "servicing."

BO, here is a place where you could really help by encouraging the seed capital to bring this new innovative product to market faster. That would be a profitable "investment" for you! (Or any other venture capitalist.)

Big government, please stop trying to control everything. Just get out of our way. Free enterprise made this country great. Big government has succeeded only in imposing onerous restrictions, which always only inhibit innovation and economic progress.

BO, you don't seem to understand that capitalism is the foundation of our success. It is the source of income to each and every American, and thus the source of taxes to fund the government. The more successful each and every one of us is, the more funds are available to fund the government. The more successful capitalism is, the more taxes will be available to fund the government.

BO, if you want more dollars coming to Washington to fund the government, you only need to cut all taxes, all of them, everywhere! Regan and Bush did that. It worked for them. Just maybe it will work for you, too.

Your plans to raise, increase, and generate new taxes do not work. That has been clearly demonstrated over and over again.

Capitalism works simply because it motivates each and every one of us to work hard, contribute to society, and help to build bigger and more profitable corporations.

But all of that is not understandable to, or experienced by, BO. Therein lays the problem.

CHAPTER FOURTEEN

THE ELECTRIC GRID

BO Wants to Control This Too!

Yes, he wants to tell you when you can wash your clothes, dry your clothes, wash the dishes, and what and when you can do anything to warm your cold house in the winter or cool your warm house in the summer.

You think I am kidding? I only wish I was.

He is doing it all in the name of making sure that power is always available. And yet he wants to control when and how you use your power. He will switch it on and off as he, "The Boss," decides it is in your best interest. (Or is it in his best interest? For more and more control over every aspect of our lives?)

Remember, "We all have to make sacrifices." But BO's plan to take over the electric grid includes the ability and the intent to do all of the above and more, including shutting down your power entirely as he sees fit.

He won't tell you this. But remember one form of telling a lie is not divulging the whole truth. And at that, he is a thoroughly experienced expert.

BO plans to ostensibly justify all of this by controlling the electric grid. He will grab this new control by adding additional transmission lines all across the country, "so that power will always be available, everywhere it is needed."

Who in the hell gave him that stupid idea? It may be the dumbest of all.

If it was economically viable, it would have already been done! It is not economically viable, and that is exactly why it has *not* been done!

But don't blame good old BO. He's just repeating it (He reads it ever so well from his many teleprompters). He didn't conceive it. But whoever the "Scientific Genius" was that conceived that idea must have been educated in the same liberal college as the guys in the DOE who screwed up the solar collector mission and the windmill fiascos.

Or just maybe this is only another of BO's ruses to seize control of yet another aspect of our lives, and bite off yet another big chunk of the economy as a further step to complete Marxist/Socialist control. That frightening possibility, unfortunately, does make a whole lot of sense. He seems to relish control and the subservience to him that it engenders.

Once again, he simply doesn't understand the concept of "economic viability." In fact, none of them seem to understand free enterprise, or how capitalism works. Or why it does work so well.

Capitalism is the driving engine of our freedom. The free enterprise system is the foundation for our nation, the enabler of our prosperity, and the individual success of each and every one of us.

He apparently has never realized that he works for us. He is supposed to be doing things for us. It's not the other way around. Somehow he thinks that he can control everything. It is a "Big Brother knows best" mentality. It does not work.

Each and every one of the economic downturns in our capitalist-driven society has resulted directly from government intervention, whether it be two years of BO preaching "The worst economy since the Great Depression," and "Unless we act right now, we may never recover!" or the Fanny and Freddie actions, aimed at making it possible for everyone to have a home of their own, regardless of whether or not they could afford it. Not to mention all of those restrictions and regulations that directly impede growth of the economy.

And what do our libs do? They, as always, do not offer any solution to the problem. Instead, they step aside and attack! They attack capitalism in their full attack mode. With irrational rage!

Remember that. And then write, call, vote, and act vigorously to preserve our liberty.

If additional nationwide transmission facilities were economically viable, they would already have been implemented. BO seems to overlook the cost of installation, maintenance, and especially the enormous power losses that are part of any electrical power transmission.

His plan calls for doubling the voltage of those high lines to 785,000 volts a.c.. That just might get some of it to its destination, but it still is not economically viable. And who knows what the collateral health effects may be to all the humans and other living things in proximity to that level of energy transmission?

I once lived about two hundred feet from a 23,500

volt a.c. "local" highline. I just happened to observe a thirty volt induced voltage in that house's wiring with all of the real incoming power turned *off!*

What can you expect from a 785,000 volt a.c. power line? Even if it stays as a high, "high" line, and doesn't decide to visit a nearby plot of ground, or worse yet some poor guy's house?

And he is one of the libs who is worried about possible health damage from cell-phones!

Has he ever even asked what is the lost power in transmission lines over three thousand miles? It is a very big number, no matter how high you raise the voltage, and how many kazillions of tax dollars that you invest in hanging bigger copper wires. The power that is dissipated and wasted in such a harebrained scheme is still sufficient to power a big city or two. Who pays for that?

But libs do not address any problem rationally, examining the facts. They just want to "feel so good," because they see power everywhere it is needed as a good thing. To the lib, it doesn't matter what horrendous consequences emerge from their stupid, irrational actions. They were just "unintentional."

But BO wants to control everything. It gives him a sense of being in power. No mistake about it He is "The Boss"

(Perhaps a release of a little reverse discrimination there? Or perhaps a gigantic chip on his shoulder?)

Regardless of what may or may not be motivating him, he has clearly embraced the Marxist philosophy, which has failed miserably wherever and whenever it has been tried.

How do you suppose it has managed to infiltrate our White House?

See one of my other books, *The Anatomy of a Liberal.*

CHAPTER FIFTEEN

BIOFUELS

Yet Another Liberal Dream

Another of BO's (teleprompter) favorites is "Biofuels"!

Culturing biological organisms, translation "gooey slime," to artificially produce a fuel that can be burned in diesel buses or in aircraft engines (When mixed with an equal part of normally used fuel!)

At what cost? At what potential damage to the internal pumps, fuel paths, igniters, and other internal workings of these enormously complicated and very expensive jet engines? Or, for that matter, the pumps and injectors of those diesel school buses that are also heavily dependent on clean, clear, uncontaminated fuel for proper operation?

Vegetable seed oil, converted to a different form of "Biofuel," at least on the surface, appears to be a possibly more easily available and potentially convertible to a fuel that perhaps can be reliably burned satisfactorily. But converting edible food to drive our airplanes and school buses doesn't really make much sense.

How about that plant in Washington State that was constructed to convert seed oil to Biofuels? It's idle, shut down completely.

Why? Because it costs $270 per gallon for the incoming bioseed oil, to which you have to add the cost of processing it into biofuel, and the result, even without adding profit, exceeds the price of conventional diesel fuel, which now is at $1.50 per gallon.

The owners of that plant are standing by, and hoping (and praying), that eventually they may be competitive again, when and if diesel starts upward in price ever again.

Again, just let the free market develop or reject these options.

BO, you can be a hero:

1. Remove all the regulations that impede free enterprise, and
2. Lower all taxes, starting with renewing the "Bush" tax cuts, and dump the capital gains tax entirely!

Then step back and watch the economy burst into action. Then and only then, you can take a bow. And with it, reap the flood of tax revenues inundating you too, back in D.C., where you belong. Makes your job a cinch.

All you have left to do is strengthen our military and reduce the size and cost of the government in D.C. and elsewhere around the world. All the staff that previously enforced those onerous regulations will be out of work in a flash when you start "examining each item in the budget, line by line, and eliminating all waste," as you promised.

If you truly want some free enterprise growth advice, dump all of your Marxists advisors, and start listening to people who understand free enterprise!

You clearly didn't learn anything about it at apparently now very liberal Columbia University's undergraduate exposure or at traditionally liberal Harvard, where you apparently were very thoroughly immersed in Marxism, and somehow you believed it is better than capitalism. Why? Because you were told so by another lib.

Time to rethink that, Mr. President? You bet! Way past time!

And while you are at it, try a little humbleness. You are not God, or even the reincarnation of the Messiah. Even the guy that was sent by God was humble. It is a good quality that you might well try to emulate and incorporate in your actions. Start by a moratorium on Bush bashing. It is only yet another form of juvenile "security blanket."

Start acting like a true leader, not just an impressive Teleprompter reader.

And by the way, dump all those guys who are filling your Teleprompters with Marxist rhetoric.

In the immortal words of Mark Levin, "There I said it. And I am glad!"

There are many people who understand capitalism and know how free enterprise works. Bring them into your administration. Dump the Marxists.

As a good start, you might like to consider these candidates on your short list: Steve Forbes, Larry Kudlow, Mark Levin, Rush Limbaugh, Mark Simone, Monica Crowley, Laura Ingrahm, and all the others with valid evaluations of your Marxist-motivated Socialist performance.

Or, are you perhaps actually a "mole?" purposively injected into our White House by the radical terrorist religious leaders in the Middle East, where there are those "fifty-seven" (Islamic) "states"?

Let's hope and pray diligently that this is not the case, and that you are not yet another terrorist attack, this one that sneaked into the White House, with the aid of monstrous campaign funds, from as yet never fully disclosed sources; campaign funds from Middle East backers. Possibly carefully laundered, to disguise their true source.

Why were the sources of all your campaign funds never fully disclosed?

Could be. Same MO. Sneaky sudden attack, with no warning, and sudden destruction. This time destruction of our entire economy, not just two of the towers from which parts of the economy were once monitored.

Osama what's-his-name must be laughing out loud in his cave, or wherever he may be.

Remember BO, constructive criticism is the sincerest form of complement.You can learn a lot from those who criticize you.Unless, of course, you think that you are already superior to everyone else. Remember, criticism is also the sincerest form of flattery.

CHAPTER SIXTEEN

ETHANOL

Let's All Starve for Good Old BO!

Still another of BO's big dreams is ethanol, as an anti-knock additive to gasoline and eventually as a fuel in itself.

What's so wrong with that? Plenty. As a starter, the corn that is diverted to the production of ethanol is not available to be eaten. Consequently, the cost of corn worldwide goes up when there is less corn to eat. Eventually, there is little or no corn available for food. People starve?

Ethanol as a fuel is yet another myth. Why? Because when it burns, it yields only about one half the energy that petroleum products do. It contains only one half as many BTUs (units of heat) per gallon that the same quantity of gasoline, and other petroleum products contain.

It contains only one-half the energy per gallon that gasoline contains. Therefore, you need two gallons of ethanol to replace each gallon of gasoline. Once again, *it will never be economically viable.*

Still another, and even more serious problem with ethanol is that it is *highly hydroscopi.* It picks water vapor out of the air. The water vapor condenses to water and settles to the bottom of the fuel tank. To run, the engine fuel is drawn from the bottom of the tank.

Engines do not run well on water as a fuel (engines stop running when water is their fuel. Water does not burn). In addition to keeping the engine from running, water in the fuel combines with that ethanol and causes all manner of related problems, each of which results in extensive maintenance and intermittent, unexpected engine stopping, all by itself.

Specifically, these include clogged injectors, filters, fuel pumps, their associated fuel supply lines, and their fuel discharge lines. This ethanol usage causes all manner of problems with the workings of internal combustion engines. Problems that are particularly acute in very humid conditions, such as found in boat bilges, where their engines and fuel tanks are usually located.

Just speak with any boat owner in any marina to hear the grief and danger that he has experienced as a direct result of the onerous government mandate that 10% of each gallon of fuel must be ethanol.

And what does BO want to do? He is on a path to *increase* the ethanol content in gasoline from ten percent to twenty percent. Boaters will love that. The late Ted Kennedy would have been delighted.

Incidentally, when and if BO succeeds in raising the ethanol content in each gallon of fuel from ten to twenty percent, in addition to further exacerbating the maintenance difficulty, guess what? You will automatically also have to pay an extra five percent for the fuel you need, because the extra ten percent of ethanol is only one half as powerful as the gasoline fuel that it displaces.

Let's try it a different way. Your mileage will decrease by 5% each time you visit the pump and get that extra ten percent ethanol. That extra ten percent that contains only one half the energy that the gasoline that you are not getting displaces.

For you chemists, the ethanol does not dissolve in the gasoline, it displaces it. It mixes with it, reduces fuel economy, and screws up the inner workings of our engines, royally.

The government is mandating miles per gallon, and then reducing the power in each gallon. Typical bureaucratic snafu. They probably do not even realize how illogical and ridiculous all those onerous, plain, stupid regulations really are!

You know this whole screw up has been around for quite some time, and it is getting worse and worse. Almost a hundred years ago, it was discovered that tetra ethyl lead was a very effective antiknock additive for gasoline. It was included for years, in minute additive quantities, less than one percent.

And then came the "oh so goodie" liberals, who discovered that if their little darlings ate paint chips, that some of them got sick. At that time, the better quality and longer-lasting, better-looking paints contained lead. There was a hot competition between the better paint companies, who advertised that they were better because their paints contained lead, and the not-so-hot paint companies, who did not use lead (Perhaps because of patents?). In any event, the paint companies with the lower quality, cheaper paints, apparently won that battle, perhaps assisted by convincing the pubic, and ultimately the government regulators, to outlaw lead wherever it emerged in our society.

Notwithstanding that those little darlings that ate the paint chips, and became ill, may just have become ill from ingesting bacteria growing on the dirty window sills. Perhaps a little over reaction, but nevertheless, Boom! In simple lib logic, the word "lead" became an instant fearful word.

Incidentally, almost all of the residential construction prior to this big lead lib discovery utilized pure lead water service entry supplies. And as far as I can determine, many of them are still up and running with absolutely no ill effects.

And for years, copper piping was always soldered with lead solder, as were all of our electronic devices. No more. That lead, to the control everything lib, is verboten!

Do they ever question where the evidence is? No! Just full speed ahead. They like the feeling of "being in the know," and instead of explaining the why, they simply look down at you, and proclaim, "You just couldn't understand."

And these are the guys we have elected in Washington. That in itself is far more frightening than lead. When the control-and-regulate everything libs triumphed, lead was banned from gasoline, and MTBE was hurriedly substituted as an antiknock fuel additive.

It turns out that MTBE was even more lethal, under certain conditions, and was quietly phased out, with no admission of guilt from our liberal, regulate-everything friends.The farmers pushed in ethanol, in its place and lobbied for increasing it from the original five percent to ten percent, and now they are shooting for twenty percent.

A very *dumb* idea. BO, once again, you are on the wrong track! Forget about getting the votes from all those farmers, and instead do what will help the country, the greatest nation in the world. And be proud to lead that great nation. No apologies are ever needed or warranted.

So quit politicking and campaigning and start doing what needs to be done. That is the only path to your much sought after second term!

BO, are you really sure that you want to go to twenty percent ethanol? How about zero instead? And bring back tetra ethyl lead. We know that it works, for sure, and apparently it has never killed anybody, or even made them sick. It works. It works well. It *saves* fuel as a bonus over that ethanol-diluted gasoline fuel mix.

Just perhaps the lead scare is not based on fact. Why not have a serious scientific look at that too? We could also benefit significantly from some of that good old lead-based paint.

BO, be a hero: remove all of the onerous federal regulations that are strangling the life blood of our free enterprise system!

CHAPTER SEVENTEEN

EVOLUTION OF OUR MEDICAL CARE

From the "Medicine Man"

We can all learn and profit by looking at what has been our experience with medical care. When we first arrived in what was destined to become the USA, the "Medicine Man" was "Medical Care." We brought with us the ideas of a doctor, and the concept of the medical facilities that he needed to treat his patients. That worked out well (it was more effective than the Medicine Man).

In fact, it worked better and better as new advances were made in medical care, such as the EKG for examining coronary disease. EKG tests helped doctors more effectively understand, diagnose, and treat patients with coronary disease in one form or another.

That was about the same time that doctors made "house" calls and dispensed drugs from their traditional soft black leather bags, which contained all their tools: stethoscope, blood pressure measuring device, tongue depressors, etc.

The point is that they were a one man free enterprise, independent operation, in and of themselves. Completely free. Free enterprise in all respects.They charged as little as $1.50 per visit, and you paid it at the time of the visit, in cash. No bills, no collection costs, no heavy administrative burden. Simple.

You did not call the doctor unnecessarily, because in those days $1.50 was a lot of money when starting wages were less than ten dollars a week.As medical care progressed, it developed all manner of new tools. And some doctors began to specialize. And the concept of a "General Practitioner" (GP) doctor evolved from the previous doctor, who did everything, (just like the medicine man.)

As medical care improved with the addition of all manner of new facilities. Guess what? Costs went up in order to pay for those new facility improvements, and to enable additional progress for still better health care.

About the time of the "Big Depression," when FDR was inventing the concept of "pay as you go" (withholding) income tax collection, the medical care system evolved their own analogy to FDR's "Pay as you Go."

It was for the purpose of facilitating the payments due to doctors and hospitals. It started with Blue Cross, and later Blue Shield, which are both effectively a "pay as you go" for doctors' bills, and hospital and related costs, respectively.This transition was facilitated because funds were short, and somehow we Americans prefer to pay monthly, however irrational that may be.

In any case, it happened, and it worked for the doctors, the patients, the hospitals, and all of the related health care facilities. When you have insurance, "someone else pays" or at least so it seems to many. So guess what? Gone was the incentive to conserve. Whenever you wanted to, off to the doctor, whether or not it was a necessity. And often it was not.

So costs started to rise faster, along with insurance

premiums. Employers began to offer health care insurance to attract and retain their employees. And insurance rates continued to rise.

So this entire medical insurance thing, which was initiated by doctors who were having problems collecting their fees, has mushroomed out of control, with administrative costs, and profit seeking insurance companies, and health maintenance organizations, all competing to provide health care.

When Medicare was invented, it was an opportunity to pass the bill to the government, federal and state. Government seems to always be ready to take over and control everything that they can get their hands on, and medical care is no exception.

Despite the failed takeover of health care by the misguided "Hillary Plan," BO is full speed ahead on an even worse "solution." Read on!

In New York City speak, "I can't believe this is happening to me."

CHAPTER EIGHTEEN

MEDICAL CARE *A LA* VA

How We Take Care of Our Veterans!

Medical Care: BO wants to take it over entirely. Couldn't be a worse idea, even from him.

Here's why:

Medical Care *a la* VA is the closest thing we presently have in this country to the "Socialized Medicine" that good old BO is apparently advocating. Let's take a look at just how well that is working out with our veterans.

We must "take good care of our Vets." Great idea, but it doesn't just happen.

So a massive federal health care system has been established for that purpose, complete with multiple paper pushers and lots of overstuffed waiting rooms, where the vets wait patiently for hours at a time in order to be "seen" by a nurse or doctor, who ends up pushing paper into the system, and very little else.

Let's illustrate with a specific example.

A WWII Veteran that I know quite well, let's call him "Joe" (because that's not his real name), was totally disabled and was awarded 100% disability compensation after sitting in the waiting room of a VA Hospital for fourteen hours. The award, $385.00 per month (down from his monthly $1850.00 service pay during

WWII). As Joe slowly regained a portion of his health, the award was gradually reduced, and arrived at sixty-seven dollars a month.

The VA also "corrects" these disability compensation allowances for inflation annually. But only if they exceed $100/month!

Joe heard from some of his friends (not from the VA) that he might be eligible for prescription drug assistance from the VA, and sure enough he was. All he had to do was furnish the VA with the prescriptions from his own doctors, drive for an hour, and wait for an hour, when he was "seen" by a nurse, who would diligently enter a whole lot of data into a computer, and then say good-bye an hour later, when Joe was on his way for the one-hour trip home.

Following this, a few weeks later, sure enough here comes the prescriptions. Great?

Almost, but not quite. Aciphex was one of the drugs Joe needed, but it is quite high priced, and the VA doesn't "provide" that one. They have a substitute drug, which is not a generic substitute, but a "just as good" substitute, which costs less, and they do "supply" it instead.

(Or is there some manner of payback within the system from the company that markets the "just as good" drug? Could be. It seems government big wigs do much better than their legal, announced compensation would permit. But that is another part of "big government" that needs fixing.)

Back to Joe. He tried the "just as good" stuff. It doesn't work for him. In fact, it has a negative effect.

Joe has glaucoma and the treatment for that is eye drops. They are expensive, too. But the VA takes care of eyes in a different facility, also about an hour away from where Joe lives, but in the opposite direction. Joe is summoned there once a year, too.

Same routine, except here there is a doctor who takes the prescriptions for the eye drops from Joe's eye doctor and enters them in the computer, after the one-hour drive, one-hour wait, and one-hour drive home.

After all this bureaucratic paper pushing, which I forgot to mention includes filling out all sorts of redundant forms each year, what happens? The prescriptions may or may not arrive. Most recently, Joe tried to re-order some pills that he had used up, and was advised, by the talking computer, no less: "That prescription has expired and cannot be refilled."

Along the same lines, the latest eye drop prescription he received was for a quantity one third less than all prior prescription fills.

And there was a time when he received eight refills in a veritable deluge. Sort of like the farmer who got a call from the post office inquiring where they should deliver his Reader's Digest. Our farmer replied, "Put it in my mailbox like you always do." The postmaster replied, "No, no, you don't understand, you have thirty thousand copies here!"

Back to Joe. When all this started Joe was "charged" a five dollar co-pay for each VA "gift" prescription filled. That fee progressed upward to six, seven, and is now eight dollars. It used to be for up to a three-month supply, and now it is eight dollars per month.

Walmart is advertising two hundred different prescription drugs, each for four dollars per month. Or even ten dollars for three months. That would be twenty-four dollars from the VA. The VA is doing right well on those.

But wait, there's more, much more. The VA bills Joe's Medicare and his private supplemental insurance provider for each of his "doctor/nurse" visits. Do you understand just how ridiculous that is? The government is actually billing itself! And, of course, billing Joe indirectly by billing his supplemental insurance carrier as well.

But nothing is too good for our vets. We must appear to be helping them, while all the time helping ourselves from their supplemental medical insurance.

But think of all the paper that that generates, and all the great paper pushers that they can add to "enhance" their organizations!

And there is still more when Joe reached sixty-five and he applied for Social Security. They asked Joe, "What other government reimbursement are you receiving?" Now when Joe received his WWII disability award, the VA told him, "Don't ever tell any other government agency that you are receiving this."

But Joe has integrity, and so he added the sixty-seven dollars a month that he receives from the VA to his reply, which also included his civil service annuity retirement plan. When Joe replied that he was receiving civil service annuity of a hundred plus a month (for twelve years in government service) and VA disability compensation of another sixty-seven dollars a month, guess what happened to Joe? Those amounts are both considered to be "part" of Social Security and are therefore deducted from Joe's Social Security check of some whopping eight hundred dollars a month.

P.S. Joe equals this from a private retirement account after only five years as a professor!

I forgot to mention two other interesting things about Joe. He just happened to have been born in what has been dubbed the Social Security "notch." That is the two-year period where Social Security recipients receive less. Don't even ask me why those two years are not good to have been born in for Social Security. It just is.

All manner of lobbying for correction of this injustice have yielded no action, perhaps because many of them have already died and are no longer around on Election Day?

The second interesting matter that I overlooked is that on Joe's last scheduled visit to the VA he arrived fifteen minutes late. Since he had always waited at least an hour to be "seen," he expected that his fifteen-minute late arrival would fit right into the system. Joe is always unusually diligent about being on time for his appointments, and medical appointments are particularly important to Joe. So in this case, he allowed two hours for the expected half hour trip.

It turned out to take much longer to find the new location of the VA, which had moved.

The new location was in what had been a portion of town that had been condemned, everyone kicked out, their houses demolished, and "government buildings" built out the Gazooh. Almost all were vacant, except for the VA that now occupies a portion of one, complete with an adjacent parking lot, apparently laid out by some government engineer who wanted to conserve space, because it is almost impossible to get in or out of your car after you have managed to squeeze it into the very meager allotted width.

This big federal "Make Work" "Neighborhood Improvement" project had all manner of twisting and turning roads, with names no one in town seemed to have heard anything about, much less know where they were!

The VA had included a "map" of the directions to the new location so that Joe could find his way. It was a Googled map, which ordinarily would have been helpful. But this map, which came with Joe's summons to the VA, had been reproduced so many different times by different mechanisms that it was totally and completely unreadable. Even the partially legible written instructions didn't work for Joe.

So, as you may imagine, it took longer than expected for Joe to arrive. And despite the generous extra time allowance, Joe was late. Fifteen minutes late.

Since Joe had become accustomed to waiting at least an hour or more on each of his previous visits to the VA, he thought that on this trip the fifteen minutes late would simply absorb fifteen minutes of his "normal" wait of an hour or more.

Dream on, Joe. Not so. He was preemptively instructed, "Make a new appointment." He was arbitrarily given a time and date about two months later.

Incidentally, Joe also reported that the "reception" area of this newly relocated VA facility was abundantly populated by obviously new people, very obviously ecstatic about their new friend in the White House.

It was apparent that they didn't have a clue about their new jobs. The one white guy who had previously handled the whole affair by himself, without fanfare, was still there to be sure. But he was off in a corner, ignoring the "I'll show you" attitude of his new "helpers."

Joe reported that in his opinion, it appeared that the white guy was obviously just weathering the storm until retiring.

So much for change! Would you ever return to, or recommend, a private doctor who treated you with such utter contempt? Plus utter contempt from his reception crew?

It would be another matter if they were busy saving lives, or even doing efficient medical evaluations. But they were not. They are just paper pushers, moving at the usual civil service pace, slow and plodding.

I have observed that the really great doctors have really great ladies there to greet you. In fact, a very good way of determining the potential competency of a new doctor is to observe who it is that he has selected to greet you.

And by the way, on that return visit Joe also arrived early. It was lunch hour. The entire place had been "shut down" for lunch, and all those new receptionists were sitting behind tightly closed sliding Plexiglas windows, gobbling up their food and jabbering away with each other a mile a minute. All of the sliding glass "windows" were closed tight, and they were obviously not about to be opened.

So Joe took a seat in the waiting room and waited.

Is this really what you want in health care? It's a sample of what BO plans, only his version is even worse. Read on.

And forget about what his "free" health care plan

will cost you. You don't even want to know. And for what? More "VA" type health care?

After paying all that to create the VA health care system, take a look at what it is actually accomplishing: virtually nothing at all. And this is what BO is proposing as a model system to be extended to one and all?

The likely cost of providing VA-type care to one and all is indeed massive. Is paying for all that really a good approach? After all, it accomplishes little or nothing at all, perhaps even yields negative results?

But we are such "good people." We really "care." Never mind taking a rational approach that actually accomplishes something. Just "care." This is the liberals' favorite mantra.

Wake up call for all good, loyal, proud Americans. Consider the facts and conceive and implement a workable real plan, not just a pretend, make-believe, feel-so-good plan!

The VA is dissipating a fortune and accomplishing little. Are you sure you want to follow that model, BO? When you are considering that question, take a look at just how well it is working in the other countries that have installed it.

Consider, as well, that you, the patient, no longer have the freedom to select a doctor, and a specialist, and a hospital in which you have confidence.

In our present health care system (the best in the world), the really good doctors are very busy. The "not-so-hot" doctors spend time working for places like the VA to supplement their incomes. Those are very important considerations if you really want to live a long, happy, and productive life.

Remember that when you have your next opportunity to vote. And be really sure to be there, early, (and often, if the ACORN Community Organizers can afford to pay you adequately).

CHAPTER NINETEEN

MEDICAL CARE *A LA* MEDICARE

At Least Partly Free Enterprise!

Let's take a look at another example of what happens when the federal government, with help from fifty different state governments, all get involved with doling out "Health Care," each with their own "regulations" and a veritable army of "regulators."

Compared to the VA in the prior example, Medicare is better. Much better. Why? Because Medicare is not "providing" the health care in vast, federally-owned and operated health care facilities, like the VA tries so hard to do and fails so miserably.

Medicare does not own or operate any medical care facilities. They rely on free enterprise to furnish them. There are no Medicare-operated hospitals or other medical facilities, or staff doctors except the regulators who decide what procedures will be paid by Medicare and how much. These are overhead. They do not treat patients.

In the Medicare system, the health care is still provided by "private" physicians, in private facilities. Get the idea? Privately operated. Not government operated. Free enterprise at work.

Sounds much better. It is. Much better, except for a few little details, all of which are caused by the same heavy hand of too much government regulation; irrational rules that strangle the system.

Those few little details include:

1. It is going bankrupt. The administrative costs add up to forty percent of gross, (and that is all that Medicare will admit to). Any private provider would go broke in no time at all with such a burden. It's only taking Medicare "a little longer" to go broke. Sort of like the sign in the government office that reads "The difficult we do immediately. The impossible will take a little while!" Yes, Medicare is in full swing, and rapidly going bankrupt.

2. Why? Because there are all sorts of problems with it. Fundamentally, these problems all stem from the same urge to work within the system and still survive. This gives rise to all manner of creativity (translation: ways to beat the system). For example, the dermatologists that used to carve off suspicious skin anomalies developed a freezing technique that takes seconds to perform instead of hours. They do this by freezing the suspected skin lesions with a stream of liquefied gas instead of carving them away with a knife. But the fee structure in the "regulations" has apparently not yet been altered. They are doing well.

3. The "family doctors," on the other hand, are not doing well. In fact, they are being regulated out of business. In parts of the

country, they are simply closing up. If they try to work outside of the system, they are prevented from ever seeing a Medicare patient, forever!

4. Are you aware that Medicare regulates the time for each procedure, in addition to how frequently any one patient can have such diagnostic tests as an EKG?

5. And they set the reimbursement price for each procedure.

6. Don't ever forget that *forty percent* of the Medicare budget goes to Medicare "Administrative Costs." (And that is only what Medicare admits to.)

7. Allowed time with the patient is fifteen minutes, no more, no less, it appears.

8. And billing; the other day Joe tells me he happened to notice on one of the many follow-up copious paperwork forms, that his "super duper pooper snooper" had billed Medicare some fifteen hundred dollars for an examination of the first fifteen inches of his colon. Since this took less than fifteen minutes, Joe followed the instructions on the Medicare form, in a fruitless effort to determine what that was all about. After an hour or more of waiting on various Medicare administrative "800" lines and four transfers, he finally discovered that the doctor had actually been reimbursed about one hundred dollars. P.S. it must have cost Medicare more than that reimbursed amount just to push all that paper around!

9. Joe's been wondering if the doctor gets an income tax deduction for the difference between the billed fifteen hundred, and the received one hundred, as a charitable contribution?

A screwed-up system beyond all logic, in which good old BO and his buddies are apparently seeking to increase their individual net worths exponentially, as they control more and more of our lives. Is this really the sort of "medical assistance" we really need and want?

And what BO is proposing is more like the VA in the sense that the government may be planning is to provide it directly, not just reimbursing all of those private providers like Medicare does.

So much for BO's big medical plans. What's next?

CHAPTER TWENTY

MEDICAL CARE *A LA* BO

"Free" Health Care for One and All!

In the well established tradition of BO saying, "I have a plan," but never divulging any details, we can only project what we may be in for this time, when and if he acquires the absolute dictatorial control of medical delivery that he so eagerly seeks.

The worst possible (but highly likely) outcome is absolute control of all medical providing facilities. All *owned* by the government, and staffed by civil servants, all vying to achieve the next "pay grade." All diligently rewriting their job descriptions as frequently as permitted to make that next step. Or at least that is what "Joe" experienced and reported to me about what he observed and experienced, when he was a Federal Civil Service worker: a report from a firsthand witness.

BO's big plan for providing medical care for one and all comers is like the medical assistance plan currently in full swing within the VA…only a great deal worse.

Worse, because at least with the VA you still have a choice to go to the VA or to not go to the VA, and instead go to whomever you choose. Nobody forces you to go to the VA. There are still alternatives. You are still permitted to go anywhere that you may elect, as long as you can pay for those services.

And in the case of emergency care, even if you cannot immediately pay for those services, just ask the illegals from across our southern border just how well that works out.

With BO's plan, that *freedom of choice* is abolished, completely and forever.

Yes indeed, with the most likely complete control medical delivery system that BO is apparently championing, you will be forced to go to the big government for all medical needs, absolutely no exceptions.

That's it. Either you come here, or you don't get treatment.

Already, medical entrepreneurs are springing up in free societies around the world for procedures for which Medicare-driven pricing has created a thriving foreign market, because you can be "seen" sooner and because it costs less, even when you add the travel costs.

Free enterprise works. It springs up like spring flowers, all around the world. Why do you suppose that BO and all his lib cohorts are so vehemently against it? Could it be that liberal education he received at Harvard? A good possibility. Columbia? Perhaps, it seems to have turned sharply left since I was there.

BO seems to seek absolute control. Absolute control of all aspects of our lives. Like all libs, he thinks that we are all much too dumb to figure things out for ourselves. Only He, the great Messiah, can do it all for us. Big Brother knows best! BS to that!

The apparent BO medical care plan combines the worst ingredients of the Medicare and of the VA plans to yield the absolutely worst possible combination imaginable. Watch out, it may be on the way. Stop it, when you vote. And don't forget to be at your polling place, bright, bushy tailed, and early. Defeat this complete con artist at the polls. That is the beauty of our system of government.

I had the great privilege of knowing John Fentress Gardner. One of John's observations was, "You haven't as yet discovered that it doesn't matter who the president is?" I keep hoping and praying that John was correct in this matter, but I am beginning to wonder if just maybe he was not up to his usual wisdom in this observation.

But then there are always exceptions. We will see, and hope, and pray for the very best all the while.

CHAPTER TWENTY-ONE

MEDICAL CARE *A LA* FREE ENTERPRISE

Free Enterprise Works Everywhere!

Of these three chapters on different ways of providing medical care, we saved the best for last. See what you think when you make the comparison, and decide for yourself after reading and understanding the following.

If the government is really sincere about honestly wanting to provide "medical assistance," why don't they just do it? Disburse that assistance directly to each citizen for medical purposes, only as each patient decides to save it, or use it wisely, when, where, and how it may be needed.

It's called a "medical savings account."

You own it. You can pass it along to your heirs. You control it. You decide how to spend it, invest it, and use it wisely.

Use it wisely is the key difference. You have the incentive to be prudent in its use. It's not the same as the happy-go-lucky attitude of the present system, which is powered by "I am insured, so who cares how many times I go to the doctor, or what it costs? I am not paying, so who cares what it costs!"

And therein lies the problem in the present system.

Medical savings accounts are one way of "fixing" the out-of-control expenses, by letting each and everyone of us decide for ourselves how much we will spend, and where and when we will spend it. It's called free enterprise. It works wherever it is tried.

It is freedom!

Let the individual citizen have the freedom to decide where and how to spend it, "for medical purposes only."

Each individual citizen will spend it wisely. But most important of all, it will not be dissipated in the endless paper pushing of the government bureaucracy.

It's called "free enterprise." It works. It saves that forty percent "administrative" (Translation: Bureaucratic Boondoggle) cost presently strangling our Medicare. Let that citizen decide what is in his own best interest. Disburse the dollars without the middleman, and let each recipient decide how to use them most effectively.

For catastrophic expenses, legitimate emergency supplemental requests could be honored.

Better yet, in fact, forget the idea of government collecting taxes and then returning part of your money to you. Just keep it and save it for medical care. In that case, the government might be limited to satisfying legitimate catastrophic requests only.

The VA and Medicare are prime examples of how the government in Washington is intent on controlling as many aspects of our lives as they can glomb on to, and "redistributing wealth" in order to maintain and expand their control of each and everyone of us forever.

The suggestion in the previous paragraphs is the other extreme: take care of yourself.

Somewhere in between there must be a solution

that throttles the massive "administrative costs" of our out-of-control, runaway bureaucracy. Perhaps it is called Medicare, massively improved, or perhaps it is *Medical Care a la Free Enterprise*, you decide.

Health care savings accounts, to which the federal money source is directly aimed, seems like the best way for the patients.

Let's see how well that would also workout for the providers. And how about all of those "providers?"

They will flourish too!

In a free enterprise system the more capable physicians will do very well, indeed. They will be able to, and they will, equip their practices with the very best and latest technology, develop a network of medical specialists, contacts, along with excellent hospitals and knowledgeable specialists, to call in, and refer to, as needed. In short, they will flourish.

Gone will be the endless paperwork and overhead cost burdens, of billing, rebilling, arguing disputed claims with all manner of insurance companies, and satisfying endless, onerous government regularity restrictions.

The patient pays his own way. Simple. Direct. Just like he pays when he buys his food, clothes, automobiles, and everything else that he is responsible for in his life.

The physician is also free. Free to operate as he sees fit. He can spend as much time or as little time as may be needed to properly deliver the highest quality medical care to each and every one of his patients when and wherever necessary, even including resumption of "house calls" when and where needed.

He is now free to provide as little or as much as he

himself deems to be necessary, from a purely medical-need viewpoint. Not in compliance with cost limitations and in compliance with myriad dumb, onerous restrictions and regulations currently interfering with prudent medical treatment within the Medicare system.

When insulated from massive lawsuits (see chapter twenty-three), he will be free to utilize life saving measures when and where necessary to save lives. Save those same lives that are now being lost by some doctors, simply because they want to avoid potential lawsuits for "malpractice" at all costs, from fear of encountering a massive lawsuit for malpractice if they just happen to have an unintentional, unexpected "Ooops."

With this free-enterprise inspired approach to medicine, the providers have an absolute incentive to perform and perform well.

That is the most satisfying aspect of life. Medicine should not be an exception, just because good old BO wants to control, control, control!

Free enterprise works in medical care too. I know. I had direct personal contact with just such a utopian medical care system.

This situation developed a long time ago. It was in a New York Hospital environment where the physician I was seeing was the very highly respected winner of a Lasker Award for Medical Excellence, and a very famous guy, albeit (unlike BO) extremely *humble* about it all.

When he encountered a problem that he couldn't immediately solve, he would say, "I don't know what this is all about, but let's see if *we* can find someone who does?" Then push a few buttons, and *presto,* here comes the necessary assistance.

And when my famous doctor added, "Mr. Doersam is from out of town, do you think you could see him today?" The reply was always the same, "Have him come right over!"

What a truly great, dedicated doctor. What a great "network" of medical care, all working as a team, within most likely the finest hospital in the world. Completely dedicated to providing the very best medical care possible.

He saved my life and I will be forever grateful to him.

As an aside, I was being treated at the time for my military service disability. In retrospect, I really made the right decision *not* to let the VA "help" me. I would most certainly not be here some seventy years later if I had not taken the initiative to seek competent and innovative medical care.

And with BO's "plan" (whatever it may turn out to be), that option would no longer be an available alternative. It would be replaced by a system in which you are forced to go wherever *they* might choose to make time for you, to see some nurse or doctor not of your choosing, about whom you know nothing, who will spend the prescribed allotment of his "valuable" time with you all to accomplish little or nothing at all, except appearing to be ever so caring, because it is "free" to all!

And when and if you return for a "follow-up visit," guess what? You will be "seen" by whatever doctor or nurse just happens to be on duty on that day at the time you are summoned to arrive.

Nothing like starting all over each time! This entire

approach *stinks*! No matter how much pork our libs add to it, in order to ram it through Congress, against the clearly expressed will of we the people. All it accomplishes is to provide BO with more and more power.

Free enterprise works. It works everywhere it has ever been tried. It will work in medical care too. It will result in better medical care for all citizens of this great United States of America. It will cost less too! Much less. (Poof! There goes the forty percent plus government overhead burden.

And free enterprise competition will result in even more ways of reducing costs and fees even more. That's what free enterprise competition enables.

Competition is unknown in government-run operations. They are, in fact, the biggest offenders of their own monopoly anti-trust laws!

And by the way, this private medical care delivery system will drastically cut costs by eliminating all of the massive administrative costs burden; always the biggest portion of any government-sponsored and/or controlled and operated "program."

Just remove *all* of those onerous regulations and let us develop and use what we need, and we will do well.

But more importantly, medicine will advance.

CHAPTER TWENTY-TWO

MEDICINE IS ADVANCING

Free Enterprise is its Driving Engine!

Yes! Just remove *all* of those onerous regulations, and let us develop and use what we need, and we will do well.

But more importantly, medicine will advance.

We are in the very beginning of an entirely new approach to medicine, with the new methods and innovations coming as a direct result of the recent startling breakthroughs and discoveries in genetics.

Improved understanding of what is going on inside our bodies, with associated entirely new and more effective medical cures. All as a direct result of recent genetic discoveries, which are opening up the way to this vast new era.

When unimpeded, science will provide innovative new ways of accomplishing new and exciting things. Lift the restrictions on the drug companies and let them be free to innovate and develop drugs that save people, and bring them to market without the fear of having them yanked off the market if two or three people just happen to crap out in a group test of ten thousand. Perhaps they were destined to crap out anyway, or perhaps it was caused by a totally different problem, such as something as unrelated as an ingrown toe nail.

Open up the gates that are restraining doctors and

scientists and let them be free to operate without all of the many present restrictions that are greatly restricting progress. And if something does go "Ooops," publicize it widely, so everyone will understand what happened, and why that cannot happen again.

Free enterprise. Privately financed medical progress. We all want to live longer and more vigorous lives. Big government, just get out of our way! Here we come!

Stem cells are yet another medical approach that has tremendous potential. Can anyone imagine what might be possible if you could regenerate any part of your body by simply injecting stem cells?

All manner of problems could be solved in new and creative ways with this powerful new tool.

BO, lift the restrictions on stem cell research.

There is no need to abort pregnancies simply to harvest stem cells. There is an ample supply from umbilical cords that presently end up in the discard bin. Why on earth would anyone be adverse to using them?

Once again, it seems that big brother is blocking progress. Just get out of the way and watch the progress we will make without you in the way.

CHAPTER TWENTY-THREE

MEDICAL MALPRACTICE INSURANCE

Eliminate it?

These days, all medical doctors, hospitals, manufacturers, and drug creators are all targets for possible massive multi-million dollar lawsuits. Consequently, they all pay substantial portions of what would otherwise be income and/or profit for "malpractice" insurance. These medical facilitators are a huge and very vulnerable target for lawsuits, under present laws and regulations.

It is relatively easy for a talented "Slip and Fall Lawyer" to select and convince a jury of the awful tragedy of a patient who has suffered from a medical "oops" of one sort or another.

Now that is reasonable, providing the settlement is also "reasonable," as well. But claims have dramatically zoomed off the charts, not because the claims are reasonable, but rather because the lawyers receive, on the average, a fat fee of 40% of the gross settlement (the client usually pays all "costs" as well).

Speaking of motivation! The recipients of these huge legal fees, these guys really have it made. They are even advertising on TV and radio for possible additional claimants on their group "Class Action" lawsuits.

They use the highly persuasive line, "You won't have to testify in court" to draw them in, en masse!

Now there is something that really needs to be changed.

It is something that either needs to be eliminated altogether or drastically curtailed, in order to justify a reasonable compensation for situations when the patient did not fare as well as might reasonably be expected, and doctors are subject to lawsuits for "Medical Malpractice."

This has given rise to a thriving industry in malpractice insurance. Basically, this system is flawed and needs to be fixed. BO, take notice. Here is yet another place where you can be a real hero.

Let's go to extremes and postulate that we will immediately lift all laws on which "Medical Malpractice" is based. No more lawsuits. No more need for "malpractice" insurance. All of that presently wasted malpractice insurance premium money can now be redirected to building medical practices, hospitals, and other supporting medical facilities. Or even returned to the patients in the form of lowered professional fees.

All that money can now be redirected toward helping the medical profession instead of stealing it from them and directly inhibiting their actions, as it now does.

Instead of suing the "Be Jesus" out of not-so-hot doctors, how about making their track records public, in detail?

If they have had a whole lot of "oops," that will redirect patients to the better doctors. The not-so-hot doctors will fade away, without enriching all those Slip and Fall Lawyers.

Even those lawyers will likely find more useful work, perhaps defending crooked politicians. Publicize the track record of each doctor, and his accomplishments, as well as his "Oops." In no time at all, the word will get around about where to go for good care, and the not-so-hot ones will gradually find other careers, perhaps in even more interesting pursuits!

That's the extreme example. It is presented to illustrate the waste in the present system.

The reason why it is an artificial solution is that it totally ignores the reasonable compensation to which the patient should be entitled. Let's look at some alternatives.

It would cost a lot, and yield very little net compensation, if we put the VA in charge. So we can forget that as a potentially viable approach.

In a less extreme example, at the very least, let's rein in the runaway lawsuit awards by limiting the awards to a more reasonable maximum permissible settlement limit.

By limiting maximum settlements, the recipient would be adequately compensated. The cost of malpractice insurance would dramatically decrease, and these Slip and Fall lawyers would still be raking in a holy fortune.

Perhaps the BO administration would like to tax that fortune the same way Wall Street bonuses were retroactively taxed confiscatoricly by BO.

One thing for sure, good old BO is making a whole lot of new, and very powerful new, "friends."

Back to the subject at hand, by limiting the maximum possible settlement award, it may perhaps encourage the fast talking Slip and Fall lawyers to be a little less aggressive; since they will be forced to be satisfied with a good deal less than their current multimillion dollar fees.

I prefer the "extreme" version. But you know we have to be politically correct in these matters. To do that, it seems we must placate the libs and their leader BO.

So let's compromise and go after limiting the maximum possible award. After all, the lawyers are still doing pretty well, with a million or two every now and then.

And while you are at it, BO, how about eliminating all "Class Action" lawsuits.

Those suits that yield fortunes in fees to the lawyers, but very little to the plaintiffs, other than the burden of filling out and filing endless paperwork!

All manner of useful suggestions in this chapter for you, BO. Better go back and read it again.

PART III:

BO's "Accomplishments" Where Has He Taken Us?

In the next chapters, we will take a look at what BO has "accomplished" in his first one hundred days. It starts with all those promises. It continues with what he has accomplished, what he has not accomplished, and then takes a look at how his actions, and lack of actions, may affect our future lives.

CHAPTER TWENTY-FOUR

TAXES

Raise them!

Whatever happened to BO's promise, "I will cut the taxes of 95% of all taxpayers?"

Did anyone ever believe that? It will never happen. Instead, 100% of taxpayers are already experiencing massive tax increases. This BO lies.

He lies intentionally to gain his own ends. To promote Him, the "Boss." When it comes to taxes, he is scrambling around all over the place to find new ways of increasing them on every one of us, as fast as he can.

It is the source of his power.

Tax, spend, and control. That is his MO in his stealthy attack on all our freedoms. Control. That's what it is all about.

One of his newly discovered taxes is the "Value Added Tax," or "VAT," which is so despised in Europe. It taxes "Value Added" in each of the manufacturing processes, for each and every product, from raw materials to market.

And good old BO is trying to implement it, in a stealthy manner, by calling it "Cap and Trade"! See chapter thirty-two.

CHAPTER TWENTY-FIVE

SPEND

BO is the Biggest Spender Ever!

"Spread the wealth around."

This is one of his promises that he has kept. He thinks that taxing the rich, and spreading the wealth around, are things that need to be done; done at least to get him elected. The fact that it doesn't work that way is a little detail that he conveniently neglects to mention, or perhaps he doesn't understand it.

But he has committed more of our hard-earned tax dollars to "programs" in his first 100 days than all of his predecessors (combined) since our founding. Yes, that is a promise he has fulfilled. Spend, spend, spend!

He enjoys that. It gives him power, so let's spend some more, of the next generations' taxes. Spend more and more until we are all bankrupt, and the government can step in and nationalize everything.

Isn't that the ultimate objective of Marxist/Socialist "Utopia"? Tax and Spend. Those are his biggest two accomplishments, so far.

CHAPTER TWENTY-SIX

THE FIRST ONE HUNDRED DAYS

My "Accomplishments"

As I write this, the news last night reported that (in lock step with his co-conspirators in the House and Senate, Nancy and Harry), the Democrats had decided to ram the BO Health Care Plan through the Congress without any debate.

Without any opportunity for the opposition to present amendments, or even filibuster this monstrous, wasteful, medical care plan for each and every one of us. BO now is even closer to having even more of the dictatorial powers he seeks so aggressively.

This BO "Massive medical care plan for one and all" (which is still undefined as of mid-October) is simply BO attempting to take over yet another major part of our economy.

Socialism, *a la* Karl Marx, is obviously his ultimate goal.

It is the big BO absolute takeover of the entire health care operation in the USA.

Is this the way our federal government system is supposed to operate? Or have we been hijacked unwittingly, yet again, by some very subversive element, perhaps Islamic Terrorism, this time from within?

Marxist/Socialism is a disease. Apparently, we were naive in thinking that it could never attack and infect us. But it has. Big time.

Good old BO has "requested" a full hour of network TV on his one hundredth day in office to tell us all about how he "accomplished" all the things that he promised in his campaign. All within the first one hundred days, just as he promised.

And his eager, enthusiastic accomplices in the press will comply, albeit. It seems they are somewhat concerned about their loss of revenue, (estimated to be twenty-six million dollars) as a direct result of BO commandeering some of their high revenue advertising slots.

And that concern is interesting in itself. Apparently the news media still thinks that BO encourages free enterprise.

They are naive. He doesn't. He is out to destroy it completely.

In fact the Marxist/Socialism that he is championing and aggressively propagating so prolifically throughout this great nation, is in direct opposition to all free enterprise. It's all about him. "I did this." I am the boss. "It is I who will make all the decisions," and on and on.

Seems the whole idea of doing something for the country, for the benefit of the people, and for the future of this country never occurred to him, because it is totally absent and unknown in the BO mantra.

Before the big forthcoming speech, let's take a look in the next chapters at some of the things that BO has already triggered.

CHAPTER TWENTY-SEVEN

THE ECONOMIC DOWNTURN

"I Inherited that!"

Yes, in BO speak it was all Bush's fault. "I inherited that!" He is big on passing the blame to Bush, but he most certainly encouraged the population of America to be fearful of what might happen, with his constantly repeated rhetoric of "The worst economy since the Great Depression," and "If we don't act right now, we may never be able to recover."

And then ramming his "stimulus" through Congress, in the dead of the night of the very same day that the Congress received it for the first time. All fifteen hundred pages of it! It was passed before anyone had a chance to read and understand the bill.

It was "passed" in the dead of night. And worse yet, BO signed it! Most likely without ever reading it either!

Is this what you expect from your president? It's never happened before. Let's make sure it never happens again.

One member of BO's team of co-conspirators reportedly proclaimed, "After all, you should never waste the opportunity for change that a big 'crisis' provides." I'm not all that sure that he even intends to help our economy to ever recover. If you define recovery as the reinstallation of free enterprise. That is totally contrary to the Marxist/Socialism nationalize-everything path to socialism that BO very obviously seems to be leading us down.

In my view, he caused it single handedly and intentionally in order to create the crisis that enabled him to take over the entire economy and turn us against ourselves, with him in control of the new Marxist/Socialist state.

But everyone is entitled to their opinion. That's mine.

It will be fun to see just how valid it is by his performance during his "last" 1,361 days, still remaining in the balance of this first nightmare, and most certainly his one and only term in office.

I have faith in the American people, and God.

And remember, we the people still have the power to decide whether or not to vote him in for that so sought-after second term, for which he has never stopped campaigning.

One term it is, unless, of course, all those ACORN efforts pay off from the fifteen billion dollars that BO dumped in their laps, at our expense.

Oh, did I forget all the other illegal new BO voters that he will welcome from across our borders?

ACORN may even instruct them on how to vote, and pay them for each poll they vote at. I have heard that ACORN may be perfecting that.

And with their old "community organizer," now ensconced in the White House, who knows what might happen?

But we must all hang together, "von by von!" as one of the wags in the navy used to say.

CHAPTER TWENTY-EIGHT

HEALTH CARE

Nationalization in Full Speed Ahead Mode!

Nationalize it. We have just seen why this is not a good idea. But BO hasn't figured that out yet. In fact, I am becoming convinced that he never even tries to figure things out by himself. Like all libs, he just accepts what he is told.

It has been reported that there was an interesting error that resulted in his reading the wrong speech to the right audience. It seems that his teleprompters had, in error, been loaded with the speech he was scheduled to give the next day, to a different audience. It was all loaded and presented mistakenly for today's speech.

Although it was a totally different topic, and a totally different audience, he reportedly plowed right ahead and read it as eloquently as he always does, without apparently realizing that it was a different audience, and the wrong speech.

Can you imagine what the liberal-biased press would have done with that if *Bush* had done the same thing?

But BO can do no evil, and consequently, it got little or no coverage in the press. Perhaps you may not have heard about it at all.

This BO guy has a lot on his mind; but sooner or later he is going to have to figure out a lot of important matters, all on his own, and not just read from his teleprompters.

It would be ever-so-nice if that process got underway before he takes over and destroys health care.

CHAPTER TWENTY-NINE

THE FINANCIAL INDUSTRY

Nationalization in Full Speed Ahead Mode!

Note that BO has never had any prior executive experience of any kind. But he steams into two of the largest corporations, fires their executives, pushes them into bankruptcy, rewards the unions handsomely, screws the bond holders, wipes out the stockholders, and ends up creating the biggest mess you could possibly ever imagine.

Is that just an honest exercise of normal presidential authority? Or is it an illegal, impeachable offense? Perhaps it is a matter of which president does it? But these are certainly very unusual and unprecedented actions, to put it politely.

Seems that he may be starting to keep his promise to, "Spread the wealth round."

"I inherited that from Bush" will simply not work as his excuse this time. We, the people, are beginning to wonder how this all came about. Elections count. Seems we all need to be reminded of that.

The "nose of the camel is already under the edge of the tent." Translation: he has destroyed and acquired a good portion of the top industrial and financial organizations already. He seems to be hellbent on grabbing the balance.

Just watch and see if I am right on this one, too. I sincerely hope that I am wrong. But Marxist/Socialism is in power. And Marxist/Socialism does not "tolerate" free anything. Control, control, control is their mantra.

Sort of like, "Change, change, change, we will never have change until we have change!"

And all our liberal friends, who have absolutely no sense of humor, are so consumed with being "politically correct" that they are totally unaware of how hilariously stupid that sentence is.

Yes, he took over the banks by buying up their various securities in various forms. Some of the banks, mainly the smaller ones, refused to accept the government's offer of "assistance."

Remember Ronald Reagan's immortal observation. The most frightening twelve words in the English Language are, "I am from the government and I am here to help you!"

The banks that refused the government "assistance" were the lucky, and prudent ones, who figured things out for themselves.

Of the banks that took the government "bait," some have changed their minds, and are ready, able, and eager to reverse the deal. What does the BO government say to them? "Not so fast, you may need it in the future."

This may be true, but they want out now, and they have the funds to get out now.

BO's new regulations state that you have to pass their "Stress Tests" that all banks will now be subjected to before we will even "consider" not owning you. And who configures the stress test? The very same government that refuses to take back the "assistance" that the banks say that they do not need.

Watch out for this one! When the "results" of the "stress tests" are made public, as BO has stated that they will be, Kaboomb!

What a great way of triggering a run on some of the banks, just like the Great Depression. This one, once again, could be triggered by our very own President BO!

After all, the great Senator Chuck Schumer, Democrat from New York, reportedly triggered just such a run on a small California bank.

Why do you think the banks want out? Could it be that they see the dark clouds of Marxist/Socialism descending only too stealthily, which will inevitably stifle all free enterprise? Or do you suppose that they saw what BO did to some of the other financial institutions with his Marxist/Socialists "control all the money" policies?

BO, take another look at the advice in Chapters Three and Four, and then call Steve Forbes and have a little chat with him. It will be very helpful.

He will educate you on all the things that neither Harvard nor Columbia apparently know much about. It is called free enterprise capitalism. It is the prime mover that has made this United States of America the greatest nation ever on the surface of this earth!

You need to understand that, BO. See if you can explain it to the first lady, too.

CHAPTER THIRTY

MANUFACTURING INDUSTRY

Nationalization in Full Speed Ahead Mode!

Grab Detroit as a starter. But look at all the things that lie ahead in our new Marxist/Socialist BO-controlled society.

Start out with GM, and then screw Chrysler into a contrived bankruptcy, in which your union workers jolly well get the best of the deal, while all others are treated poorly. And that was after you summoned them to Washington to be excoriated by your liberal friends in Congress.

Reread Chapter Five and see if you can figure out exactly why Marxist/Socialism is a very poor idea, indeed.

Embrace free enterprise. It would be a great change for you; but well worth the effort. Start thinking for yourself and stop following blindly what Karl Marx preached. Socialist/Marxism does not work. Sooner or later you will figure that out. Sooner would be better than later, for you as well as this great nation that you seem bent on aggressively destroying.

Free enterprise has made the USA the greatest

country in the world. Why would you seemingly want to deliberately destroy it?

It doesn't make sense, unless, of course, you are simply a pawn of some other movement, perhaps terrorist conceived, and liberally funded? (Pun intended!)

Terrorists in action, yet again? This time, right here at home, in the very center of things?

CHAPTER THIRTY-ONE

"CARBON CREDITS"

Yet Another Onerous New Tax!

Our global warming hero, one Al Gore, the "inventor" of the internet, seems to have created yet another hoax: "Carbon footprint!"

It is doing well for Mr. Gore. In fact, it has yielded him a fortune.

From a new tax standpoint, which is all that it is, it is a winner: a new source of funds for the treasury. And look out...it is you, the people, who will pay that new *tax*! And tax it is, despite the sneaky, stealthy means that are being used to disguise it.

BO wants you to think that it is a burden on the eveel *big business*, and indeed it is. But all business "costs" (and that includes taxes, new and old) are passed right along to you, the consumer. Businesses do not "pay" any tax. It is one of their costs. That's the way free enterprise works in a free society.

Under this sneaky new tax scheme, it seems that each "polluter" will be assigned an allowance, which is shrunk each year to "encourage less pollution."

Aside from the fact that "global warming is a completely liberal generated *hoax*, there is no basis for the government declaring carbon dioxide a "pollutant." After all, every living being inhales air and exhales carbon dioxide. Are we all subject to the new tax as polluters?

And don't forget that all of the things that grow, the ultimate source of the food we require to exist, all of those things that grow, they need carbon dioxide as the main source of their health.

This simply has gone too far. It needs to be stopped right now.

When fossil fuel is burned completely, it generates heat and discharges water vapor and carbon dioxide up the smokestack or out the exhaust pipe. Water vapor condenses and then rains back to the surface.

Carbon dioxide is also produced by humans and animals. They inhale air, which is mostly nitrogen and oxygen, and they exhale the nitrogen, some unused oxygen, and some oxygen that has been added to carbon to produce exhaled carbon dioxide.

All the things that grow take in carbon dioxide and produce oxygen. In this way, there is a balance between things that grow in the ground and things that walk on that ground.

This is an arrangement conceived and designed by God a very long time ago. But our control-everything libs have decided to interfere with this long time, and very well working arrangement. They want to control it. Apparently they don't trust in God, or just perhaps they don't agree with the plan, which has been working well for thousands of years.

In any case, they have proclaimed that carbon dioxide is a "pollutant," and must be taxed in order to restrict, limit, and eventually ban it altogether!

Do you have any idea how hilariously stupid banning it all together really is? What are we supposed to do? Stop breathing?

Might as well stop breathing, because there will not be any food to eat anyway.

It's interesting to note that libs don't believe in God. Perhaps they don't like competition.

BO likes the idea. It is a new source of taxes, and of course, it gives him even more power to control it all!

In any case, libs want to "control" this process as well! Mr. Gore has established a brisk market in the trading of "carbon offsets." It seems that when you exceed your annual allowance, you have to buy offsets. There are even libs "planting trees" as saleable carbon offsets.

And the European Union is following along, getting a piece of the "action" as a new source of tax revenues. And that exactly is all that it is; yet another onerous tax. A tax on "big business," those "evil" guys; but guess who pays it, in the end? You do. The consumer.

More "tea parties?" You bet!

Carbon dioxide has officially been declared as a "pollutant" by the US Government, no less (EPA ?). And why is it a "pollutant?" Because it is a "greenhouse" gas! Whatever that means. The libs love to assign names to things that "explain" everything. These "politically correct" names are never questioned. It is the way it is. I was told so (by another lib).

Let's take a closer look at this entire "global warming" thing, because that is why the libs invented "green house gasses" and how carbon dioxide has become the liberal designated culprit.

Let's start with the lib claim that, "The temperature

has increased by 0.7 of a degree Celsius over the last one hundred years."

(It is interesting to note that as the years go by, the lib mantra is always "the last one hundred years.")

Just how accurate are the temperature measuring devices that we have now? And that we had a hundred years ago? And just where do you take your measurement? At the North Pole? Or do you stick your thermometer up the south pole? Seven-tenths of a degree in over a hundred years indeed!

And thirty years ago they were screaming about "global cooling." And they don't consider that the sun's output is not always the same, as recently measured by temperature increases on Mars (and even similar evidence from very far away Pluto!)

Do you really suppose that all those pollutants are traveling to Mars and Pluto? Or is it just a variation in the output of the sun, as all rational thinkers conclude?

But try to tell that to that lib in the White House, who is delighted that he can embrace a new source of tax revenue. A new tax on you!

But this doesn't stop our liberal friends that at this time have managed to launch multiple satellite "trains," circling around all parts of the earth, disparately trying to "prove" global warming!

That has been going on long enough to yield results, but we haven't heard any. Why? Because they are "inconclusive." Translation: There isn't any "Global Warming," but if they tell us that, *Poof!* goes their government funding.

CHAPTER THIRTY-TWO

CAP AND TRADE

It is Yet Another Tax on You!

BO is embracing it as a great new source of revenue; what he really enjoys the most!

It really is just a very thinly disguised, "back door," sneaky way of implementing a Value Added Tax ("VAT" for all of you libs who may have never heard of this European Marxist/Socialist monster tax nightmare invention.)

Let me describe why "Cap and Trade" is nothing more than a VAT!

Cap and Trade is being "sold" as a way of helping to "clean up the air," and stop the (non-existent) "Global Warming" and "Save the Planet." All things that libs embrace fervently. So they gobble it up.

They have generated all sorts of "politically correct" words to describe it. "Carbon footprint" is one of their favorites. "Carbon emissions," and "carbon credits" are still others. One wonders if they understand that carbon is prevalent throughout all humans, animals, and in fact carbon dioxide is the most essential ingredient in plant growth.

And yet, these dumb libs who believe everything that they are told (by other libs) insist on trying to "control" everything in sight! Dream on! But it seems that we may be stuck with it (BO relishes it).

Notwithstanding the myth of global warming, this Cap and Trade, is simply a backdoor way of sneaking in a VAT while no one is looking.

Sort of like when one burp said to the other burp, "When no one is looking, let's you and I sneak out the back way."

Here's why it's unworkable. Cap and trade imposes "permissible" greenhouse gas emission allowances for each member of every industry. These permissible allowances are reduced successively each year, ostensibly to "clean up the atmosphere."

But when you inevitably exceed your progressively declining "annual allowance," you have to purchase "credits."

The system is already ongoing in Europe.

There is a brisk trading market in credits. Sort of like the stock market. Prices up and down, all over the place, as a function of supply and demand! The European exchange is complete with bid and asked prices, and traders "earning" commissions on each "sale."

With emissions increasing as we need more power, and need to burn more jet fuel, this cap and trade allowance is going down each successive year.

This is a formula for total economic disaster.

The ultimate result is that we will all once again be carrying around clubs to bop our next dinner, the way we all started out as cave men!

Is that what you really want? Or is it let's just punish the other guy; you know, all those big power companies and airlines, and all those evil "Fat Cats."

Well, I have a surprise for you libs. It is those big corporations that supply the jobs, the new innovative products, the advances in medicine, and all the other ingredients that we are experiencing, and enjoying, since the day we no longer carried those clubs.

Libs don't realize that "turning back the clock" as a form of sacrifice to "save the planet," is a stupid and utterly unworkable idea.

The planet was here for millions of years before we arrived and will be here for millions of years after we are all long gone!

How about just saving mankind from crazy self centered Socialists/Marxists that want only to destroy the free enterprise system that made this the greatest country to ever be on the planet?

Like all their lib mantras, "Save the Planet" is a dumb idea. In fact, it is a very dumb idea.

The only winners are apparently the very same Socialists/Marxists that are hell bent on destroying free enterprise so that they can rule the world forever.

How well did that work out with Joseph, Adolph, and Benito? And they were the ones who almost made it. Cap and trade will destroy free enterprise big time!

Let's take the power companies, world wide, as an example. When they are forced to purchase credits, who do you suppose pays the bill? You guessed it, they don't. They simply pass it along to you!

Let's try another example: an airline that exceeds its meager allowance has to purchase credits. And who do you think will pay that bill? You, the traveler, of course.

Are you beginning to get the idea? This is simply yet another additional tax on *you!*

But energy is the driving force in our entire economy. So we will need more and more of it in order to be able to propagate and develop new and innovative products, eat healthy foods, have medical care, and all the other things that we have come to enjoy and, for the most part, take for granted as our right.

In order for that progress to continue, we will need more power.

Power is the driving engine of our free enterprise economy.

But this "Cap and Trade" (fancy name for VAT), reduces the "allowance" for all industry, each and every successive year.

Even a fifth grade school student, with reasonable skill in arithmetic, would very easily figure out that that creates an unsustainable upward spiral in the "cost" of "credits!"

Why do you suppose BO hasn't figured this out? Or perhaps he has, and he is intentionally leading us down yet another path, which is knowingly and purposely designed to destroy our entire economy, so that he, BO, can actually destroy America, and thereby control and rule the world forever?

How well did that work out for Benito, Adolf, Joseph, and all the others who have tried it and failed miserably?

Everything, every product you use, needs power in one form or another in order to produce it.

Energy is the common denominator of all manufacturing. Each step in the manufacturing process consumes energy. When that is effectively "taxed," *presto*, you have the equivalent of a "Value Added Tax," a VAT.

By the way, that VAT is thoroughly despised by the Europeans, where it has been in full swing for well over forty years and utterly despised by all Europeans.

VAT taxes the "value added" each time a product

moves up a notch on its trip to the market. An insidious tax to be sure. One to be avoided at all costs.

Perhaps BO will figure that out. But don't hold your breath while you are waiting.

And this "carbon credit" thing is worse. Why? Because eventually, the yearly declining carbon credit annual "allowance" goes effectively to zero! Now just what is it that you are trading? Tree planting? It is destined to self destroy from its inception.

But think of all the new revenue that it provides for the government. And it is all coming from those eveel big businesses!

No, it is not! It is coming from you, you dummy!

But libs do not think for themselves to figure things out. They just "trust" the experts. Those are the other libs!

CHAPTER THRITY-THREE

PATENT LAW MODIFICATION

Bet You Haven't Heard About This One!

Yes, it has been recently reported that BO has already instigated changes in Patent Protection laws, which significantly diminish the opportunities available to the emerging inventor for receiving swift patent protection in order to bring his invention to market in a timely manner.

This is yet another insidious step toward the complete destruction of our free enterprise system. It effectively throttles research and development, the driving engine of new and innovative products.

Bet you hadn't heard about that one.

Get the idea, this guy is a Marxist, and everything that he does with his accomplices, Nancy and Harry, and all those other complicit dems, seems to be directed solely toward gaining, strengthening, and retaining his Marxist/Socialist dictatorial powers forever!

The patent office is already backed up. There are presently some eighteen thousand applications in the queue.

It takes about three years to process an application.

The "changes" that BO has reportedly already

installed effectively choke all possibility that an individual inventor, with a novel good idea, can reasonably expect to receive adequate patent coverage that will enable bringing that new product to the market in a reasonable time.

Why do you suppose that BO throttled this creative free enterprise initiative so swiftly in his first one hundred days in this backdoor action? He hasn't mentioned that, in any of his many endless campaign, teleprompter-reading speeches.

CHAPTER THIRTY-FOUR

"GREEN" LIGHT BULBS

Yet Another Disaster!

BO is once again determined to control our every move.

This time he is mandating "green" light bulbs.

He, and all his fellow libs in Congress, seem to thrive on controlling more and more of our lives by taking away more and more our freedom, our free choice, to decide what is best for us, not being forced to do what BO forces us to do…ad nauseum.

This time he has really stepped in it! He has gone too far. Much too far.

Let me tell you why.

He has reportedly ordered that all the lights in the White House be changed to "green" light bulbs in order to "set an example" for the forthcoming mandated banishment of the good old incandescent light bulbs that serve us so well.

What do you suppose that Thomas Edison and Irving Langmuir would say about that?

(Let me see if I can give it a try.)

This is yet another example of BO going off half cocked, without knowing what in the hell he is doing! He, like all libs, acts on feelings. And it just "feels" that it is such a great idea.

As usual in these impulsive decisions, he has not

bothered to learn even enough to make a rational decision.

In fact, it seems that he has not discovered, or considered, the obvious consequences.

The ultimate consequences are perhaps even more dramatic than the MTBE to Ethanol screw up in the anti-knock gasoline additive fiasco.

Here are a few of the reasons why "green light bulbs" are a very poor plan indeed, even in the White House.

Those long tubular fluorescent lamps that have been so successfully used in factories, and industrial, commercial, and domestic installations, for years, work very well. They do save power. That's the main reason that they were created by innovative free enterprise-driven inventors.

In a capitalist-driven state, this is the sort of innovation that flourishes and has made this the greatest nation on the planet!

The reasons why this form of generating light have been so successful are all "capital-driven," they provide more and better light for lower cost.

Let's dig a little deeper into the reason why.

They run on alternating current. Now, it so happens that the power company charges the customer for the amount of power used, plus a delivery cost.

But alternating current is a little tricky. The amount of current that flows in each of the sixty successive cycles a second reacts differently to two (of the three), different main types of load (Stay with me, we're getting there).

Motors have iron and magnets inside. The current has to magnetize the iron on each cycle, and this takes time some fraction of the cycle. Depending on the design of the motor, it may be more or less. There is a name for it. It is called the "Power Factor" (Hold on we are almost there).

Now the fluorescent lamp also has a power factor. But it is in the opposite direction. It is capacitive, and stores and returns the extra power that it does not use, so that the inductive load of the motors can utilize the stored capacitive load of the fluorescent lamps.

This works well in the factory, where there are a whole lot of motors and fluorescent lamps. They balance the power factor, reduce electricity delivery cost, and reduce metered electric power.

The customer is rewarded with lower energy cost. The power companies are rewarded with lower delivery costs.

Get the idea? Free enterprise creates all manner of innovative solutions.

As a bonus, fluorescent tubes have a longer operating life, as long as they are not turned on and off frequently. That dramatically shortens their life. And that is the main reason that they are purposely, frequently left in the "on position" twenty-four seven.

When the inductive motor load is the same as the capacitive fluorescent lamp load, the grid distribution is ideal.

If you are wondering about that "third" main way that power loads function, it is called resistive. All by itself, it has a power factor that doesn't lag or lead in each cycle. All by itself it is ideal. Incandescent lamps are pure restive loads by their very nature.

We have already noted that fluorescent lamps can last a long time, and that they can save power in the industrial environment. To a certain extent this carries over to the domestic environment, where however the inductive, motor load, is usually lower so that the savings, and other benefits are less.

There are some other very serious problems. Remember that the alternating power swings plus and minus for each of the sixty cycles per second. This was created as a way of facilitating power distribution. It enables the distribution of power at lower cost, but it makes fluorescent lamps flicker. The flicker is driven by the alternating power cycles.

But the human eye reacts poorly to the flicker. In fact, in a drafting room lighting situation, some of the designers developed serious eye problems as a direct result of this flicker.

To mitigate the flicker, you may have noticed that most fluorescent lighting fixtures have two separate tubes. See if you can guess why this is? You've got it if you guessed that while one tube is going "on" the other is going "off" so that one is always coming on. This reduces the ill effect on the eyes, but it does not cure it entirely.

But BO and his liberal Socialist/Marxists want to "change" this too. In fact, they want to do this by controlling it. And therein lies the problem.

Some very clever marketing fellow has taken the fluorescent tube, curled it up in a roll, arranged to have it screw into an incandescent lamp socket and *presto,* "green" light bulbs.

While it is never easy to figure out what BO is going to do when he makes one of these "I have a plan," proclamations; it appears in this case that he intends to have all of the presently installed incandescent lamp bulbs in the White House replaced with those curlycue "green" ones.

And they have even passed a law that it will be illegal to manufacture incandescent light bulbs after a certain date.

One of the main advantages of fluorescent lamps is that because they are long, they emit light that reduces shadows.

Green bulbs concentrate the light source. Poof, here come those shadows back!

The inventor of the green lamp may have not considered that one, and perhaps he also neglected to consider the following as well.

Another problem with green bulbs is that they cost over ten times as much as the tried and true incandescent lamps.

Sure, they last longer, but only if you don't turn them on and off frequently. That may be possible in commercial/industrial applications, but it doesn't work out too well in a well disciplined domestic environment.

When fluorescent light tubes collect dust, dirt, and moisture from the air, they sometimes experience starting problems when turned on. When this happens, usually all that is needed is to wipe the outside surface clean. Just how will you clean a "green" lamp? Perhaps run it through the dishwasher? What if it breaks in there? See the following!

Read on to learn more about the mercury hazard.

Each fluorescent lamp contains a tiny drop of mercury, in order to provide some electrically conducting mercury vapor to enable the current to flow and energize the fluorescent material coating on the inside of the glass tube.

Mercury is a very bad material in lib land.

Not withstanding that one of the most popular childrens' Christmas toys once was about a pound of mercury! You simply dropped it on the floor, and *presto,* a kazillion little shiny round mercury balls scattered in all different directions.

The little recipients of this gift then expend the next hour and a half or more chasing each drop and returning it back to the original single blob, by rolling one drop at a time back to the company of its buddies.

Despite the fact that this apparently was a very successful toy, that apparently never made anyone sick, mercury has now been banned.

As a result, it "has to come out" of fluorescent lamps too.

That doesn't work. They don't conduct and light up without their electrical conducting mercury vapor.

So we will "fix" that! (Our lib friends have declared.) We will simply reduce the amount of mercury in each tube by a half!

Guess what: The new "Green" fluorescent tubes last less than *half* as long, or even less if turned on and off frequently.

Now the intent in cutting the mercury content by a half was to reduce the mercury heading into the waste stream. The result, with more frequent failures, is that more mercury actually enters the waste stream.

Did you notice that you were stuck with paying for twice as many of those "green" tubes? Each one proudly marked with green end caps?

But wait, there's more, much, much more.

Mercury has been designated to be a hazardous material. When one of those tubes breaks, you are not permitted to pick up the pieces. You are required to call in a fully qualified "Haz Mat" disposal ream, all dutifully clad in white disposable uniforms to scoop up the pieces and clean up the mess.

Just how they recapture the mercury vapor is not apparent.

Can you imagine how "busy" all of those guys and gals on the Haz Mat teams will be when people start accidentally dropping their fancy curled up "green" light bulbs.

And how much will that clean up cost? And who pays for that? Is that the sort of government intervention that we need and really want in order to have "better" lives?

CHAPTER THIRTY-FIVE

THE FIRST 100 DAY PRESS CONFERENCE

A Press Charade!

If ever there was a charade, all pre-choreographed, that was it!

I estimated that in the one hour "press conference," there must have been between two hundred and six hundred "annnd, ahhhs," BO's most famous habitual phrase. It is one of the characteristics that I admire least in BO.

But it is somewhat better than the liberal sprinklings of "You Knows," that libs repeat over and over again, ad nauseum.

What specifically was strange about the press conference?

Plenty!

For a starter it was clearly a "puff piece," intended only to boost the stock of BO, in the minds of all of his followers.

Did you notice that he was reading the (prepared) answers to the questions from his Teleprompters?

Did you notice that the sequence of questioners was all pre-arranged?

Did you notice that all of the "questions" were not really pertinent to what is going on?

Did you notice that he didn't seem to know any of them?

The prime example was the guy sitting directly in front of him, in the front row, who he addressed with "Where are you?"

Suppose the Press Corp had actually been doing what they are supposed to do, asking the questions that we the people would like real answers to?

Perhaps he would have gotten some of these:

What are you doing about the Taliban? What about the variously reported (from fifty to a hundred) nuclear weapons stockpiled in Pakistan? Are the Taliban invaders going to be allowed to acquire those stock piles of nuclear weapons?

Why do you want to nationalize the financial industry? Why are you taking over major industries in Detroit? What plans do you have for similar industries? Why do you claim that you are cutting taxes when you are raising them across the board?

The Bush tax cuts resulted in fifty-four successive months of economic prosperity, in spite of 9/11 attack and our necessary response. Why do you want to let those tax cuts expire?

Isn't that just another tax increase?

Have you faithfully abided by your oath of office, which includes honoring the Constitution?

Why do you want to nationalize health care?

All these things that you are nationalizing, how does that benefit the people of this United States?

That's a sample of what the press is supposed to be doing.

They aren't.

Time to open your eyes and listen, and then ask questions, to see what is really going on.

As a fun game to increase your ability to be aware of what you are hearing, how about listening carefully to the radio and TV commercials?

No end of contradictions there. One that is pushing a lawsuit class action for people who have taken a certain prescription drug with fatal consequences, urges you to call an 800 number free! Now, if you are dead, just how are you going to do that?

Still, another is advertising a health care Medicare supplemental coverage plan, with the straight-faced line that says, "This is the only Medicare Supplemental Health Care Insurance plan, endorsed by (us)!" We are endorsing our own plan. Good grief, how dumb do they think we are?

Good experience. My sixth grade teacher taught that to our class when I was eleven years old. And I have thoroughly enjoyed analyzing the commercials ever since. It's also good practice for the things that libs like to tell you, too.

Great fun. Great laughs. Diametrically opposite to what liberals do in life. Libs neither question anything or laugh when told a joke. They are missing a lot of fun. Perhaps they don't know the difference, but they are great followers, and they are always politically correct, to be sure!

I think that means they always do what they have been told (by other libs), that that is what they are supposed to do. Who knows?

When applied to those never ending campaign speeches of BO, this intense listening that we learned in sixth grade yields all sorts of impossible contradictions!

Let's face it; he does not tell the truth. He lies. He does the opposite of what he promises. BO lies and our freedom dies!

And to finish off that big press conference, there was one last question, the longest and easiest of all, which BO very likely may have also actually written all by himself. When he said, "Wait a minute, I have to write this down," and then started in on the pre-prepared, Teleprompter-displayed "answer," it was apparent that the whole press conference was a pre-planned, carefully orchestrated and rehearsed charade.

It was simply a great opportunity for all of the fawning press to fawn even harder.

With Pakistan possibly about to lose control of their reported Russian-supplied nuclear stock pile to the Taliban; with North Korea firing long range ballistic missiles over our Japanese ally's mainland; with the Cap and Trade thing going berserk; and all the other things that the press might legitimately be interested in, why do you suppose that not even one of those topics was mentioned?

Time to can the press?

In fact, it is well past time to can the press. And we can do that by simply not buying their product. It's already started. Let's give it a little shove, by an absolute complete boycott of the liberal press print and video!

And while we are at it, let's not bother to pay to see all those liberal biased movies streaming out of Hollywood one after another!

If you really want to know what BO "accomplished" in the first 100 days, ignore the big puff news conference, and read the preceding chapters, again and again, until you really understand what this Marxist/ Socialism takeover is all about that BO is perpetrating on each and every one of us.

PART IV:

Where May BO Really be Taking Us? And Who May Benefit?

If you have been having trouble sleeping after seeing what he has already done to you, you will really have even more gruesome nightmares when you start seriously listening and wondering about what perhaps lies ahead in his master plan.

And it does seem to be a master plan, meticulously thought out, extensively planned in detail and sprung suddenly and unexpectedly.

Isn't that exactly the same way that the 9/11 attack was? Stealthily planned in detail, and launched as a big unexpected surprise! This one could be even bigger! That's the worst case? No, it could be even worse! Read on!

But first let's take a look at the other extreme, the "Best Case" possibility. The best case is a little more promising, but not much more. In the "best" case explanation for the BO actions, BO simply doesn't think for himself. He missed that great sixth grade teacher. Instead, he was "educated" to accept whatever the libs told him. Perhaps they just took control of him and greased him into the White House, and that was that.

Let us all hope and pray that that is the case. Better pray really hard.

Now somewhere in between is what may be actually in store for us. The following chapters attempt to offer some of those various possibilities. Some are more likely than others. Unfortunately, none are very attractive.

The chapters ahead strive to put some observations and some extrapolations into perspective to see where good old BO may really be heading.

Feel free to add to the list of possibilities and discuss them all with your fellow citizens to your heart's content. But if you are already one of the curious readers of my other books, you already know how to take that initiative!

CHAPTER THIRTY-SIX

BO IS STILL CAMPAIGNING

Why do you suppose that is?

BO is zooming all around the world, still in full campaign mode. Still bashing Bush, and our country, and apologizing profusely for the awful USA everywhere he goes.

Do you suppose he thinks he will become the dictator, not just of the USA, but of the entire world? Sure seems that way to me, at least. The bloom is off the rose, as the saying goes, at least in Germany and France.

Even the Chinese are laughing, while the North Koreans, and the Iranians, are thumbing their nose at his actions. When does he work? When is he actually in his oval office, making decisions? Being briefed on those nuclear warheads in Pakistan; the plans of the Iranians, with their reported seven thousand enrichment centrifuges running twenty-four seven; the North Koreans, with the same objective; and in fact all of the important things that we citizens have a right to expect from their president?

After all, he works for us. It's not the other way around.

And don't even think of getting me started on his "Oops," all over the world. He is the laughing stock of all that he addresses.

CHAPTER THIRTY-SEVEN

WHAT'S REALLY HAPPENING?

What if?

Yes, What if? The question that scientists like to ask most often when considering a new problem.

Following that scientific method.

The first step is what do we know for sure, from our observations and experience?

1. The Radical Islamic population of the world wants to rule the whole world!
2. The Radical Islamic population of the world has declared all out war against all of us non-Islamic "Infidels," Christians, and any and all others, but especially the Jews. Their long time hatred and many wars fuel that urge.
3. The Radical Islamic population of the world truly does want to see all of us "Infidels" dead.
4. The Radical Islamic population of the world is waging an all-out war against all "infidels," wherever we may be on the surface of the planet.
5. The Radical Islamic population of the

world regards it as and in fact calls it a "Holy War."

6. The Radical Islamic population of the world strap bombs to themselves, and detonate them in crowded places to blow up innocent people, indiscriminately.
7. The Radical Islamic population of the world are sneaky in their actions. See above and remember 9/11. They like to attack suddenly and unexpectedly. Sudden, Sneaky, Unexpected, Surprise Attack is there M/O, (Method of Operation).
8. The Radical Islamic population of the world has been quietly and massively infiltrating non-Islamic countries around the world, as demonstrated in Germany, England, and the USA.
9. There are credible reports from former regular members of Islamic mosques that subversive activities prevail within those mosques, under the cover of religious freedom.
10. Specifically teaching the younger generation to pretend to be loyal to the USA, while all the while really teaching them to annihilate us, when the opportunity is arranged and that opportune moment arrives.
11. So that they can conclude their Holy War by annihilating all of us infidels, and rule the whole world for ever after.
12. Many Americans have not yet recognized this threat. In fact BO has just decreed that

> "The War on Terror," is no longer permitted to be used by his accomplices in the Marxist/Socialists dominated press.

So what other observations can we make?

Well, BO is farther to the left than any other president in our history. He has clearly demonstrated that he really is a Marxist/Socialist.

During his campaign for the job, he referred to the "fifty-seven" states of the USA. There just happen to be fifty-seven Islamic states. He has been whizzing around the world consistently criticizing the USA.

He has an Islamic middle name (That we are not permitted to use). He doesn't speak coherently without his teleprompters. The source of his massive campaign funds is largely undisclosed. He wants to control everything. And when he gets control, it seems that he deliberately destroys it.

All the while telling us what he has done, and how great he is. But what he "tells" us is not what he is doing, or apparently even intends to do.

He lies. He lies intentionally! Why do you suppose that is? Our "Savior? I think not! How about our destroyer? Fits much better!

If he were intent on destroying us from within, how do you think he would go about that? How would he be acting? What would he be doing?

Yes (unfortunately), it fits much better than we would like to admit. It seems that we may have even made a major mistake in electing this guy. Have we indeed installed a "Trojan Horse" in our midst, intent on seeing us, all of us infidels, dead?

Regrettably, we may have to recognize that; yes we have!

Is this yet another terrorist arrack? This one from within our very own White House? Or is he simply another product of our own educational system; so overstuffed with liberal Marxist/Socialists professors, spouting off total nonsense about centralized control of everything in sight (at exorbitant tuition prices), apparently led by those Harvard "elitists?"

And for the most frightening possibility of all see the next chapter.

CHAPTER THIRTY-EIGHT

THE END?

We must be alert to this possibility!

The USA has nuclear response capabilities located strategically throughout the world. Without divulging any classified information, those response facilities include numerous nuclear powered submarines, each carrying numerous missiles, and each missile has numerous separately targeted nuclear warheads. So much for our navy.

Then there is our air force. They have nuclear retaliatory capability, too. As well as the aging fleet of the giant B-52 bombers, there are some newer assets: including the B-2, the F-22, the (forthcoming) F-35, and other weapon systems. Our air force also has defensive measures, in the form of missiles. So do the navy and the army.

Then we have an army. They are pretty powerful, too. Nuclear tactical weapons, ground-based and airborne, are all part of their capabilities. In fact, all of this is well known, clearly understood, and appreciated by just about everybody in the world.

And that is the reason we have been relatively safe from nuclear attack for a long time. A time long enough that it seems we have forgotten that we are a prime target for nuclear annihilation.

Our ally, Israel, has not forgotten. They are well

aware of the immediatc threat to their tiny homeland, from the radical Islamic movement; specifically, the nuclear bomb production activities in Iran.

And good old BO seems to have dumped Israel under the bus. BO wants to "talk" with the leaders of Iran. Except that that didn't work out too well with Chamberlain, even when Germany had a designated leader: Adolph.

But to whom do you speak to in Iran? Which "leader" of the constantly quarrelling factions? And what makes BO think that talking will really make a difference?

How well is "talking" with Castro and the other south of our border dictators working out? Don't even mention Mexico. This BO guy is becoming the laughing stock of the entire free world.

Our nuclear retaliatory attack capability has kept us safe from nuclear attack for years.

Fear of retaliatory measures, that we are capable of delivering, and that we would retaliate if and when being the recipients of a "first attack," all of that signals to the radical dictators of the world: "Don't dare mess around with us, Buster!"

Other countries around the world already have, or are, acquiring nuclear capability.

The risk of a sneaky surprise first attack is escalating.

BO's response, or more correctly lack of response to the threats from North Korea when they fired their new long-range ballistic missile right over our Japanese "ally," and his ignoring the North Koreans and Iranians, full speed ahead with their fifteen hundred and seven thousand (respectively) reported centrifuges running twenty-four seven, enriching nuclear material for production of nuclear weapons; all of this is more than a little disturbing.

In fact, it is downright terrifying!

But it gets worse. There's more; much, much more! BO is not only "president," he is also our "Commander-in-Chief." Probably the one most important duty of our Commander-in-Chief is to give the "okay" for the use of nuclear retaliation in the event of a preemptive first strike, such as a sneaky, unexpected, sudden nuclear attack, on, for example, total elimination of six or more of our largest cities.

For those of us that remember 9/11, we know exactly what that means. A sneaky, unexpected, sudden attack with absolutely no warning!

The "nuclear football" is always in attendance with BO, wherever he is. Time is of the essence. Minutes, seconds count. Immediate response is needed. It is all pre-targeted and set to go. But the final "okay" has to come from the Commander-in-Chief. Otherwise, no retaliatory launch.

So, it seems we are absolutely dependent on this fellow, whether or not we like that arrangement. We are further troubled that he seems to have trouble knowing where his aircraft are, when some "total stranger" apparently dispatched a couple of them for a photo shoot over the Statue of Liberty. His reaction: Who, me?

But I digress yet again. Back to that nuclear football! What if? Yes! What if he cannot bring himself to say go? Or an even a more terrifying possible scenario: What if the radical Islamists have deliberately installed this guy in that slot: as their modern day version of the "Trojan Horse."

Installed him there for the one and only purpose of being certain that there will be no nuclear retaliation? After all, he is our Commander-in-Chief. As such, he and he alone is the one and only source of the "okay" to launch.

For this reason, when the president is temporarily anesthetized or otherwise incapacitated in a medical facility, he, the president, turns over his powers, temporarily, but completely to his designated next-in-line, viz the VP.

That's an awesome responsibility that BO has. We can only hope and pray that God gives him the power to exercise it as rapidly as necessary, and wisely. It seems that he is accustomed to doing things fast; now all we need is a prompt and wise response.

For some of us, the prospect of BO in charge of nuclear retaliation is even more frightening than his economic takeover of everything in sight, starting with ownership of our entire economic system.

He seems determined to totally destroy the economy. Just perhaps he wants to destroy our nuclear retaliatory capability, too. He has already stated that he wants to "reduce" our nuclear weapon reserves.

But in typical BO speak, he hasn't said what his "plan" is to accomplish that either. Let's all pray, perhaps he really just doesn't know what he is doing.

SUMMARY/ CONCLUSIONS/ RECOMMENDATIONS

What have we learned?

Every good engineering report has a Summary/Conclusions/Recommendations paragraph or two at the end.

So here goes:

What have we learned?

1. Elections have a meaning. It is important for each and every one of us to participate after learning as much as we can about the two candidates, and after making a carefully thought-out selection. "He is so handsome; he is red, white, yellow, green, (or even) black," or "I believe his completely impossible promises," are all very poor reasons for deciding who you will support and cast your valuable vote for. "I don't like either candidate, so I am staying away from the polls," is an even poorer excuse. You are supposed to compare the choices and select the best of the two! That's how an election works. No candidate is "perfect," so it is up to each and every citizen to first of all vote at every election, and

to vote intelligently by choosing whichever candidate is the best. That is how our great country works and thrives with free enterprise as its driving engine. Your own individual freedom is a component in that driving force. Don't stop exercising it!

2. Do not believe everything anyone tells you. They may be trying to sell you something. Used car salesmen are good examples. Politicians are even better examples. They are trying to sell you something, too: Them!

3. Participate in every election. Get involved, talk with your friends and "strangers." Remember; "strangers" are friends that you have not yet met.

4. If you are dissatisfied with the direction in which the president is sending Congress, or if you clearly perceive that it is in the wrong direction, call, write, e-mail them, each and every one of them, and encourage all your friends (old and new) to do the same. Remember the president and all the members of the Congress work for us. It's not the other way around.

5. BO has promised to do a whole lot of things that all sounded really great. He convinced a whole lot of people that he, and only he, could do all those wonderful things. That's how he got elected. It now is becoming very apparent that he never intended to even try to implement any of those promises. He just wanted to be elected.

6. In fact, with a very few minor exceptions, BO has very intentionally and deliberately done exactly the opposite of what he promised. He lies. Either he is very dim-witted, or he knows that he is lying and doing it intentionally.

In the famous quote of my favorite drive-thru bank teller (in response to my query, "Did you here our leader's noontime speech?"): "What is he promising us today?"

BO thinks that he, and he alone, all by himself, is destined to take over and control the whole world. Designated by God? Except he doesn't even seem to believe in a God. Perhaps he doesn't like the idea of competition.

Off to the Appendices; they are great, too!

APPENDIX A: HOW DID ALL THIS HAPPEN?

And How Can Our Freedom Be Restored?

"All This" being virtually the complete destruction of our freedom, and with it the individual initiative to figure things out by ourselves. These are the uniquely American qualities that our founders realized really are gifts from God. Gifts that each and every one of us brings to our culture at the instant of conception! Individual initiative and freedom are the driving engines of the creativity and innovation that made America the greatest country in the world.

Individual initiative and freedom create and sustain free enterprise. It is sustainable forever, as long as it doesn't receive any "help" from the government.

It is the driving engine that has allowed Americans to become the greatest country ever to exist on the surface of this earth. The insidious counter culture that started some fifty-plus years ago has taken over by what can only be described as a lazy, "just send the welfare check to me" attitude of let "Uncle Sugar" provide.

It has never worked anywhere it has been tried. And

it has been tried in a whole lot of places. Always by "leaders" intent on eventually ruling the whole world.

Sound familiar? It is. Could that be BO's objective, too? It seems that way. He is even still campaigning in every country he whizzes through.

And, by the way, apologizing profusely for the past "sins" of America, and implicitly promising to fix it all when he becomes their new world leader; translation: "dictator."

But those Europeans, Russians, Cubans, and other south-of-the-border countries have all heard this bunch of lies before. It is unlikely that any of them are going to fall for that a second time.

But here in America, this is the first time ever that we are being subjected to it, with such force. We are also more vulnerable because of those fifty-plus odd years that our entire education system has been taken over by liberals, "teaching" the "virtues" of centralized government control of everything.

That is what happened in Germany, Italy, Russia, and all the other countries where it took roots: the prelude to the coming disaster, the overture to the tragedy about to unfold before our very eyes.

It has been going on here, too. Big time. For over those same fifty-plus years of "teaching." And Harvard is perhaps the self-appointed leader!

Perhaps BO picked it up there? Or was it my very own beloved, formerly highly respected Columbia University?

Socialism is an insidious disease. It sounds great; but it does not work. Gullible students are easily infected with it. In many cases, it is apparently incurable.

If BO is as bright as he seems to think he is; why

do you suppose he hasn't been able to figure that one out all by himself? Perhaps one of the forty-seven plus tsars that he uses as his very own security blanket will do that for him.

This "counter culture," which can only be described as very evil sprits working furiously to destroy the American God-given spirit, could be the next part of this book.

But:

1. BO is not the solution, he is the problem, and

2. That subject deserves a book of its own, including all manner of exciting new topics, such as chapters on: Why Would You Ever Want to Be "Politically Correct" Anyway?; Innovators, Creators, and Entrepreneurs vs. Liberals, Marxist/Socialism Really is Kaput; What is it that Makes Liberals so Arrogant?; When, Why, and How did it Happen that the Press Stopped Reporting the News, and Started "Making" Liberally Biased Propaganda?

Make your own list. It will be a great book, too.

It really has nothing to do with this BO guy, except that it seems he is the living image of a Marxist/Socialist/Liberal that is full-speed ahead to destroy the very fiber of America's unique free enterprise-driven success.

In the meantime, let us champion a real free enterprise-loving American, who believes in, and is inspired by God, has some real conservative executive experience, but most of all puts her love of this great country ahead of her personal ambitions: Sarah Palin!

APPENDIX B FREE ENTERPRISE VS. MARXIST/SOCIALISM

Is there a difference?

Yes, there is a difference, a very big difference. Apparently BO has not figured that out yet. That is our first problem.

Free enterprise is totally and diametrically different from Marxist/Socialism. They are completely incompatible.

You can have one or the other; but you cannot have both at the same time!

They cannot co-exist. They are completely inimical to each other.

Apparently, BO has not figured that out yet, either.

That is our second problem.

The insertion of Marxism/Socialism into our own free enterprise democratic government that BO is perpetrating, clearly demonstrates that he simply doesn't understand free enterprise; and therefore, does not realize the extent of the destruction that he is perpetrating.

Unfortunately, there are apparently many supporters of BO that don't understand these factors either.

So let us examine the situation to see if we can educate them all with the hope that they will vote more intelligently in the next elections (Even his black supporters, who must really be disappointed by his performance to date).

BO might benefit as well, but he seems to be clueless and hopeless when it comes to understanding free enterprise, or even thinking for himself, without his teleprompters, and he is an awfully far-left communist that just may be difficult to convince that just perhaps, he really isn't the second coming after all.

But let's give it our best!

Here goes:

Even animals are motivated by having accomplishments.

This was clearly illustrated by experiments with pigeons at Columbia University, where the birds were trained to inspect electronic diodes. I kid you not. The diodes to be inspected were presented one after another. The pigeons looked for defective marks, selected one of two buttons to push with his beak to either reject or accept each individual diode, and the next one appeared if the bird was right. They were faster and more accurate than humans!

If the bird made an error, guess what? The lights went out and the bird was deprived of his work. He paced around, mal-contentedly, impatient to go back to work.

Eventually, the lights came back on, and the process was resumed, with the bird more accurate and even more motivated than ever.

What is the message in all of this?

Simply that everyone, even a pigeon, is motivated by having a sense of accomplishment.

Accomplishing a worthwhile result builds self-esteem in humans (as well as pigeons).

Self-esteem is an essential, albeit a delicate and easily destroyed essential element, of all human (and pigeon) success.

Now let's have a look at the other extreme: totally devoid of self-esteem. The "welfare" state, where the victim simply does nothing. He is completely unmotivated, he is useless, and he knows it. He has no satisfaction from doing a good job. Even a pigeon needs to know that he has performed a useful task!

Now, let's take a look at what happens to individual people who are completely liberated from all government controls and even religious oppression!

A great example of this is seen in the actions and accomplishments of the first arrivals in this great new land of ours.

Can you imagine the challenges that those first settlers of our great nation experienced when they first arrived here?

They were really motivated.

It was life or death, every day.

And by the way, they had to believe in God!

And look what they accomplished!

They created the greatest country in the history of mankind, in a very short couple of hundred years, complete with a Democratic Republic, as set forth in a Constitution, which has provided the basis for success at all levels of government for this great country!

And BO wants to ignore the Constitution and insert unworkable Marxist/Socialism for the very free enterprise system that we fought so hard to define in the Constitution, and that has served us so well.

The reason that Marxist/Socialism can never be successful is that it seriously limits and constricts individual freedoms. It controls what individuals can do, or not do, in every aspect of their lives.

Control, control, control, sound familiar?

(If not go back to page one and give it another try!)

The American Constitution recognizes the *God-given freedoms*, that each and every one of us bring with us at the instant of conception! Those freedoms are from God! And no one, not even BO should ever even think about trying to take them away from us!

In essence, God says:

"Go forth and do your best at whatever you are inspired to choose as your contribution to humanity, during your brief stay here on earth, this time around."

"Go forth and do your best. If you need help, just ask, and you will be inspired to do the right thing!"

"Do whatever inspires you, and do it the best that you can."

"And by the way there is another fellow deep below where you are. Look out for him. He is trying very hard to control your every move with very evil intent. I am battling him, and I need your help. Please help me to win that battle with him, and all of the other perverted souls that he has he has already entrapped with his evil promises."

Which side are you going to choose?

My dad, who was truly a great musician, created a wonderful inspirational anthem for the famous poem, "Once for Every Man and Nation, Comes a Moment to Decide, for the good or for the evil side!"

Remember Robert Schuler's immortal quotation:

"All things are possible, when you believe!"

You can aspire to be an artist, a musician, an engineer, a doctor, a minister, even a politician, or heaven forbid, yet another lawyer in a free enterprise society.

And it was entirely your free choice in the pre-Obama free enterprise-driven society.

Not any longer.

Our new self-proclaimed, Socialist/Marxist "boss" is slamming all those doors to different opportunities shut in our faces, one after another.

Anyone inspired to go into banking these days?

How about starting a new auto manufacturing company?

Or even becoming a medical doctor? All that work and for what?

BO is set on dictating the rewards behind each of those doors, and regulating the Be Jesus out of what we can and cannot do in each and every one of our lives, in whatever we may choose to do.

What about being an entrepreneur?

You've got to be kidding!

With all of the regulations and taxes, why would anyone want to do that?

Motivation? American dream? Success? Self-esteem? *Poof!* All gone in the BO Marxist/Socialist state.

But don't blame BO!

Blame the people who voted for this monstrous disaster. "We the people," blew it big time. We, who voted for this guy, without ever figuring out that all his "promises" were not really ever going to happen.

In fact, he has done exactly the opposite of what he promised us he would do!

Either he is doing it on purpose or he must be incredibly stupid.

Is there a difference? The end result is the same.

And he never did describe what was in that "plan" that he keeps referring to.

Yep, time for a change, a real change this time.

In the 2010 upcoming election, we have an opportunity to dump all those liberal Marxist/Socialist, Democrat, and/or Republican followers, of BO who are so intent on destroying free enterprise, controlling every move of each and every one of us, and spending us into oblivion for generations to come!

At the next election, let's bring back the free enterprise, thrifty conservatives that understand free enterprise, cut spending, and *cut taxes* across the board, so that we can once again enjoy a flourishing free enterprise economy, overflowing with opportunities for everybody!

(And so we can achieve and enjoy all the bounties of freedom described in this book.)

In short, let's have a 2010 House cleaning, no pun intended, because we need to clean house in the Senate too!

Let's make it easier for the 2012 arrival of Sarah Palin, when we will enjoy some real house cleaning from the White House on down, starting with all those tsars!

APPENDIX C: SARAH PALIN: 2012!

Let's Make it the Biggest Landslide Ever!

Our liberal, heavily-biased press has very sharp eyes.

They are especially good at detecting any talented, emerging, potential conservative challenger to their liberal Marxist/Socialist agenda.

All challengers, but particularly potential conservative presidential candidates, are major targets to be annihilated, quickly.

They have perfected a pattern of attacking and destroying anyone who has conservative ideals that might differ from their Socialist/Marxist mantra.

A good example is found in what the press did to Newt Gingrich. They recognized him as a winner and attacked him viciously, even before he emerged as a candidate. They creamed him with lies and vicious personal attacks, and apparently did succeed in at least attenuating his drive to the White House.

We see the very same, vicious, untrue, unjustified, personal attacks, currently in progress, attempting to cream Sarah Palin, in the same manner.

This is sort of a good omen, because they apparently have recognized that she, like Newt, is also an intelligent, extremely capable conservative, who is motivated to become president in order to serve the country.

Not like BO, who very obviously is motivated only to serve himself, the "Boss."

See the difference?

Sarah is just like Newt in this essential ingredient, for any great, potentially successful president of this great United States of America.

She is in good company (with Newt)!

The good news is that Sarah Palin seems to be even more motivated by these harsh, untrue, challenges from the liberal press.

No signs of caving in there.

Quite the opposite. She is more motivated than ever.

What a great, personal sacrifice she is making for each and everyone of us in this effort.

Do you realize that for the rest of her life she will be a constrained target, for one and all, in the liberal press? (To take pot shots at her.)

She is certainly aware of this, and she is determined to press on and do what is right for our country, because she understands that there is a mission to be accomplished!

She is determined.

She is obviously inspired by those good spirits.

We already know that she believes in God.

That should be a prerequisite for all of our presidential candidates.

Now that it is clear that she is a splendid candidate for a 2012 conservative landslide, let's take a look at the future, and see what she may have as "competition" for the job.

BO is doomed to failure.

If you don't understand that by now, go back to page one, and start all over again!

By then Hillary will have broken away from BO.

She is bright enough to know when to abandon a sinking ship, and even Hillary is having problems tolerating the massive Socialism/Marxist takeover that BO is instigating, not to mention his massive swings around the world, apologizing profusely about the "awful and unjust" USA!

She is quite apt to "declare," and end up swiftly becoming the Democratic candidate, proclaiming, rather explicitly, or implicitly, that "I am the first female candidate" for the job.

Not unlike BO's implicit claim to be the first black, which he has used so powerfully to thoroughly intimidate all of those fearful of being branded with the "R" word!

So Hillary may very likely be the one who replaces BO as Sarah Palin's opposition.

Better lookout, she is ruthless, she stops at nothing when it cones to achieving her goals, and you can bet that she would like nothing better than to be back in the White House as our first female president.

Watch out Sarah, look at the fate of Vince Foster, and the many similar opponents that she vanquished with dispatch.

Hillary is a good deal more experienced, capable, and intelligent than BO.

In fact, she does right well, without all those Teleprompters!

Oh, did you notice that that great speech that Sarah Palin delivered early on in the last presidential campaign?

It was totally extemporaneous! Her Teleprompters were either purposely "sabotaged," or crapped out all by themselves!

In any case, Sarah never even blinked an eye. She delivered the entire speech directly from her heart, with passion and enthusiastic conviction!

Teleprompters? Who needs them?

(Only BO, that' an easy one.)

She not only understands what needs to be done, but she is passionate about accomplishing it for the benefit of all of us loyal Americans.

Not like BO, who it seems to be only seeking self-aggrandizement, as in his medical care "plan," for one and all where he is apparently completely oblivious to the majority opposition, and trying to ram it through Congress by very devious, sneaky means, while no one is looking.

There is still another admirable quality that Sarah Palin has: a sense of humor, which is sadly lacking in BO (and all libs!)

She also knows what needs to be done and how to get it done.

She is not afraid to do it.

She knows what is right for our country and has the courage to do it for our country, and not as payback to corrupt political pressure groups, such as ACORN! And the corrupt Chicago political machine that helped to install BO.

She believes in God.

She is not for herself; she puts our country first.

She tells the truth.

She does what she says she will do.

She keeps her word.

And she has shot a moose or two!

(Do you have any idea what a large animal that is?)

How long do you think it would take her to decide whether or not to send additional troops in response to a specific request from the Commanding General in the field fighting a war in accordance with her instructions?

When, if ever, will BO finally get around to that?

And remember that nuclear football?

Which one would you (and all of our potential adversaries, all around the world); trust most, to give the "okay" to retaliate?

The courageous lady who loves the United States of America (and shot the Moose), or BO, who seems to lack both love of country, and the courage to decide, even to grant the general's urgent request?

That's an easy one, too!

We all trust Sarah's immediate and wise, decisive judgment, over the indecision of BO.

So how about it? Let's start early and make it the biggest landslide in history!

And then we can all get back to our free enterprise businesses, while she goes to work in Washington, really cleaning up the gigantic mess left by BO.

And by the way, let's help her by doing a little house cleaning of our own in Congress in the 2010 election, so that she will be welcomed there with a conservative majority in both branches of Congress, the House of Representatives, and the Senate…when she arrives there triumphantly in 2012!

And don't forget to vote.
Be there, if you want to survive!
And if you want a free enterprise America to survive!

ABOUT THE AUTHOR

(You guessed it, he's an Engineer!)

Lincoln School of Teacher's College, from first to graduation (from eleventh grade).

Teaching debut at age eleven: his first "class" made model boats!

B.S. in Engineering and M.S. in Mechanical Engineering, class of 1942 BS, 1944 MS Columbia University's School of Engineering.

Engineering Research and Development career with a variety of companies, including: Pratt and Whitney Aircraft, The Bell Telephone Laboratories, The Office of Naval Research (as a commissioned officer and as a civilian), Sperry Gyroscope Company, Grumman Aircraft and Engineering Company, Fairchild Camera and Instrument Company, Instruments for Industry, The Potter Instrument Company, and others.

One of the founders and later chairman of the Professional Group on Space Electronics and Telemetering, of the IRE, (now "IEEE.")

Listed in various Marquis Who's Whos, including Who's Who in the World!

Specialty is automatic computer control.

In 1963, joined the faculty of "Polytechnic Institute of

Brooklyn." (Later called "Polytechnic University," that then merged with New York University) as visiting professor (and later Associate Professor). Developed and presented a new two-year Computer Science undergrad and grad curricula for the new System Science and Industrial Management Departments. Also advised some graduate students.

Extensive consulting, which lead to an opportunity to found "Com Comp Inc." in 1968. The first real-time, online, time-shared hospital information system. Had private placement and IPO Stock listed on NASDAQ at three, peaked at twelve.

Subsequently founded similar high tech companies. Currently President of Fiber Optic Sensors, Inc. "FOSI" (First on Scientific Innovation), is engaged in research and development for innovative new products, primarily to meet Department of Defense innovative requirements.

Founded Pedagogy Research Institute, dedicated to improving education.

Active in parents' activities at the Waldorf School of Garden City, New York, including co-chairman of the parents for three years. Member of the advisory committee in that school, when it was run by its creator John Fentress Gardner (Carol Gardner's husband).

OTHER BOOKS BY THE SAME AUTHOR

Yes You Can DO it for your Children…from arrival to the 'teens.

Education "101" a Doersam Observations Series # 1

Yes I Can DO it For Myself…from 'teens to college.

Education "102" a Doersam Observations Series # 2

Yes I Can DO it For Myself… College.

Education "103" a Doersam Observations Series # 3

Yes I Can DO it… Career !

Education "104" a Doersam Observations Series # 4

Yes I Can DO it… Entrepreneur !

Education "105" a Doersam Observations Series # 5

Yes They Did It…, Successful Entrepreneurs !

Education "106" a Doersam Observations Series # 6

Anatomy of a Liberal… (A greater threat than Terrorism) !

Education "203" a Doersam Observations Series # 7

†

Anatomy of a Conservative…Free Enterprise's Driving Engine!

Education "204" a Doersam Observations Series # 8

The Lincoln School of Teachers College

The Right Approach to individual creativity and "education."

Anthology of Jokes
Just Plain Fun!

Charles H. Doersam, Jr.
PO Box 927
Old Lyme, New York 06371-0927
(860) 434-9414